the

COURAGE

to be

Creative

ALSO BY DOREEN VIRTUE

Messages from Your Angels
Angel Visions II
Eating in the Light (with Becky Black, M.F.T., R.D.)
The Care and Feeding of Indigo Children
Angel Visions
Divine Prescriptions
Healing with the Angels
"I'd Change My Life If I Had More Time"
Divine Guidance
Chakra Clearing
Angel Therapy®
Constant Craving A–Z
Constant Craving
The Yo-Yo Diet Syndrome
Losing Your Pounds of Pain

Audio/CD Programs

Don't Let Anything Dull Your Sparkle (unabridged audio book)
The Healing Miracles of Archangel Raphael
(unabridged audio book)
Angel Therapy® Meditations
Archangels 101 (abridged audio book)
Solomon's Angels (unabridged audio book)
Fairies 101 (abridged audio book)
Angel Medicine (available as both 1- and 2-CD sets)
Angels among Us (with Michael Toms)
Messages from Your Angels (abridged audio book)
Past-Life Regression with the Angels
Divine Prescriptions
The Romance Angels
Connecting with Your Angels
Manifesting with the Angels
Karma Releasing
Healing Your Appetite, Healing Your Life
Healing with the Angels
Divine Guidance
Chakra Clearing

DVD Program

How to Give an Angel Card Reading

Calendar

Daily Messages from the Angels Calendar
(available for each individual year)

Card Decks

Butterfly Oracle Cards for Life Changes
Loving Words from Jesus
Archangel Gabriel Oracle Cards
Fairy Tarot Cards (with Radleigh Valentine)
Angel Answers Oracle Cards (with Radleigh Valentine)
Past Life Oracle Cards (with Brian Weiss, M.D.)
Guardian Angel Tarot Cards (with Radleigh Valentine)
Cherub Angel Cards for Children
Talking to Heaven Mediumship Cards
(with James Van Praagh)
Archangel Power Tarot Cards (with Radleigh Valentine)
Flower Therapy Oracle Cards (with Robert Reeves, N.D.)
Indigo Angel Oracle Cards (with Charles Virtue)
Angel Dreams Oracle Cards (with Melissa Virtue)
Mary, Queen of Angels Oracle Cards
Angel Tarot Cards (with Radleigh Valentine
and Steve A. Roberts)
The Romance Angels Oracle Cards
Life Purpose Oracle Cards
Archangel Raphael Healing Oracle Cards
Archangel Michael Oracle Cards
Angel Therapy® *Oracle Cards*
Magical Messages from the Fairies Oracle Cards
Ascended Masters Oracle Cards
Daily Guidance from Your Angels Oracle Cards
Saints & Angels Oracle Cards
Magical Unicorns Oracle Cards
Goddess Guidance Oracle Cards
Archangel Oracle Cards
Magical Mermaids and Dolphins Oracle Cards
Messages from Your Angels Oracle Cards
Healing with the Fairies Oracle Cards
Healing with the Angels Oracle Cards

All of the above are available at your local bookstore, or may be ordered
by visiting: Hay House USA: www.hayhouse.com®; Hay House Australia:
www.hayhouse.com.au; Hay House UK: www.hayhouse.co.uk;
Hay House South Africa: www.hayhouse.co.za;
Hay House India: www.hayhouse.co.in

Doreen's website: www.AngelTherapy.com

the
COURAGE
to be
Creative

How to Believe in Yourself,
Your Dreams and Ideas, and Your
CREATIVE CAREER PATH

DOREEN VIRTUE

HAY HOUSE, INC.
Carlsbad, California • New York City
London • Sydney • Johannesburg
Vancouver • Hong Kong • New Delhi

Published and distributed in the United States by: Hay House, Inc.: www.hayhouse.com® • *Published and distributed in Australia by:* Hay House Australia Pty. Ltd.: www.hayhouse.com.au • *Published and distributed in the United Kingdom by:* Hay House UK, Ltd.: www .hayhouse.co.uk • *Published and distributed in the Republic of South Africa by:* Hay House SA (Pty), Ltd.: www.hayhouse.co.za • *Distributed in Canada by:* Raincoast Books: www.raincoast.com • *Published in India by:* Hay House Publishers India: www.hayhouse.co.in

Cover design: Charles McStravick • *Interior design:* Pamela Homan

Library of Congress Cataloging-in-Publication Data

Names: Virtue, Doreen, date- author.
Title: The courage to be creative : how to believe in yourself, your dreams and ideas, and your creative career path / Doreen Virtue.
Description: Carlsbad, California : Hay House, Inc., 2016.
Identifiers: LCCN 2016006648 | ISBN 9781401948719 (hardback)
Subjects: LCSH: Creative ability. | Self-acceptance. | Self-realization. | BISAC: BODY, MIND & SPIRIT / General. | SELF-HELP / Creativity.
Classification: LCC BF408 .V49 2016 | DDC 650.1--dc 3 LC record available at http://lccn.loc.gov/2016006648

ISBN: 978-1-4019-4871-9

10 9 8 7 6 5 4 3 2 1
1st edition, June 2016

Printed in the United States of America

"If you hear a voice within you say,
'You cannot paint,'
then by all means paint
and that voice will be silenced."

— Vincent van Gogh

(letter to Theo van Gogh, October 28, 1883)

CONTENTS

INTRODUCTION

The Courage to Be Creative

It takes courage to be creative. I know from personal and professional experience, as I've been self-employed as an author and speaker since 1993. During that time I've learned a lot—including from making mistakes.

True creativity is channeling divine inspiration and expressing the infinite mind of God. Creativity is akin to patiently waiting for beautiful butterflies to flutter by and land upon your shoulder. Since I've taught intuition classes for over 20 years, I've also learned how to help people overcome fears and blocks to receptivity.

So, I'm writing this book for you, because I wish someone had taught *me* what's inside it when I first began my creative career. It took courage for me to write this book, as it's a memoir of my own personal writing and creativity processes. In these pages, I'm going to get vulnerable and share with you what it's really like to be self-employed full-time in a creative occupation. I will mentor you and teach you everything I know about how to have a happy and successful career in the creative arts.

Yes, it takes courage to be creative, and I will hold your hand throughout the upcoming chapters to help you muster that courage. I've experienced and overcome each of the fears about being creative.

After all, expressing yourself creatively means:

- Facing your deepest feelings and authentic truth, as they are the inspirations for your creativity

- Exposing your most vulnerable feelings publicly

- Sharing raw and real information about yourself, which may be embarrassing or unflattering

- Receiving criticism and ridicule from those who don't resonate with your work

- Confronting the possibility of your work not selling or being commercially viable

- Isolating yourself while you work on your creative project

That's why I admire creative folks. They're real, they're brave, and they're healers in their own way, because when others relate to their painting, book, photograph, or other art form, those people know that they're not alone . . . that someone else feels the same way.

If you're drawn to a creative career or you feel guided to have creative hobbies, then you recognize that creativity is a calling that can't be ignored. Even though you know the risks listed above, you're also in touch with the compelling feelings driving you to create.

Some people think that creativity is the same as making things up and imagining things. Well, that's only a small part of creativity. The larger part is being a mirror, reflecting how things are right now, and being a channel of authentic, raw emotions. Creativity is *problem solving* and inventing ways to meet needs and fix issues.

For every risk associated with being creative, there are many more blessings. All your efforts are rewarded when people tell you how your work has helped them, or you see your creative project making a positive difference.

In early 2014, my Hay House editor, Alex Freemon, suggested that I write a book about creativity. The idea intrigued me, as I always enjoyed teaching writers in my classes and seminars, at Hay House Writer's Workshops, on AngelUniversity.com, and at the UCLA Writers' Program. I also loved encouraging people to follow their purpose and passion.

But it's one thing to have an idea, and another to know *how* to bring it to life. And that's what this book is about: diving deep inside our feelings, including recognizing and healing blocks to creativity and enjoying a full-time creative career.

When I began writing this book, I knew the basic concept was to discuss the process of creativity. I knew it would be about all forms of creativity, not just writing. To bring this book you're now holding into being, I used the very creative process that I outline here and that I recommend for *you*. It's one I've used for all of my creative products and services, and it works!

I've studied and explored many pathways of creativity, and this book is my conversation with you about that topic. In addition to supporting myself and my family as a writer for more than two decades, I have a creative background that includes:

- Playing violin since I was a child
- Playing guitar in bands since I was 14 years old

- Starting my own business as a freehand window-lettering painter for local stores while I was in high school
- Having a backyard business making airbrushed T-shirts and selling them at my high school's student store
- Sewing my own and my children's clothing
- Dancing in an Eastern dance troupe and hand-dyeing my dancing scarves
- Co-designing a line of dresses and shirts featuring images of angel and ascended masters with designer Amana Nova, and an organic fair-trade T-shirt with Beckons Yoga Clothing
- Co-designing angel-inspired jewelry

Some of the most creative people I've met are also the most sensitive. Their sensitivity makes them receptive to divinely inspired ideas. Yet, that same sensitivity makes them shy to reveal their ideas to others.

In studying creative individuals' processes, I find that creativity is one-half the ability to listen and be receptive, and one-half the courage to put the creative idea into action. This is a book about both receptivity *and* courage.

It's about having the courage to be *yourself,* because the true you *is* highly creative. After all, you're the creation of *the* Creator, in Whose image and likeness you were made. So, therefore, you are creative yourself.

This is a book about how to live a more creative life, including having a career that supports and sustains you. The material in *The Courage to Be Creative* is based on several foundations:

- *Solid scientific research about creativity:* There are a lot of myths about creativity that are just that: myths. Scientists have tested theories about how it works, and you'll read the fascinating results in these pages.

- *My own process of creativity:* After writing more than 50 books and also dabbling in creative ventures involving fashion, music, jewelry, and art, I've cataloged a working method that I'll describe to you.

- *My own process of self-employment:* As a successfully self-employed person, I've learned a lot about how to stay consistently inspired, fresh, motivated, and disciplined with creative projects. (I also learned from my father's self-employment as a writer, photographer, and artist; and my uncle's self-employment as a freelance movie screenwriter.)

- *Observing my students' creative processes:* As I mentioned, I've taught writing classes for the UCLA Writers' Program, AngelUniversity .com, and Hay House's Writer's Workshop. I'll share my practical insights about how to put inspiration into action.

- *Studying successful and happy creative people:* I've met and studied countless artists, musicians, writers, and other creative types over the years. I love discussing their creative process. I've also read biographies of famous creative people, to understand *their* process. I'm including a few of their stories in this book.

Some people think that the word *creativity* applies only to writers, artists, musicians, and such. Actually, creativity is *practical*, with applications in business and daily life, including relationships, parenthood, health, and so forth.

In its purest form, creativity is the *outward* expression of an *inner* voice, vision, or idea. That's the type of memorable creativity that ends up on museum walls, on the radio, and in bookstores.

Yet, creativity for most people is more "ordinary," in an everyday sense. *Practical creativity* means the ability to solve problems in new and innovative ways. A study by the Institute of HeartMath found that highly successful people gave themselves permission to be intuitive and creative. They'd intuit future trends and creative ways to solve problems down the line (Tomasino 2007).

Creativity can help you take your business to the next level, assist your child's learning, increase your enjoyment of necessary activities like housework and exercise, and boost your self-confidence and happiness.

So, let's get courageous and let's get creative!

Part I

COURAGE DURING THE CREATIVE PROCESS

Chapter One

The Courage to
Be Your Creative Self

Some people walk around all day feeling like there's something fundamentally wrong with them. Perhaps *you* have felt that way. I certainly have. We feel stuck and insecure, comparing ourselves to those who seem to have it all together.

This is especially true if you've been sensitive or socially awkward for most of your life. Add extra points if you've been teased for being strange.

That describes my childhood and early adult life. Being raised by metaphysical parents who used Christian spiritual-healing principles in the 1960s and '70s, before such ideas were popular, made me very much misunderstood by other kids.

When I'd use words like *manifesting*, my classmates would roll their eyes and laugh. I'd get bullied whenever I'd mention my clairvoyant visions. So I didn't fit in and didn't know how to communicate in everyday plain language with others. How ironic that I'm now paid to communicate as a best-selling author!

I finally found my niche and tribe through sharing the language of authentic feelings. It turns out that many of us feel like an outsider, as if we don't belong on Earth or with other people. So, I've spent my career exploring—and writing about—these feelings and experiences.

If I'd listened to my insecurities and concluded, *Well, I need to feel completely confident before I'm qualified to be a writer,* I wouldn't have written my first book.

These days, I do have confidence and feel comfortable with my humanness. I have compassion toward myself and others, knowing that we're all doing the best we can. While I don't feel insecure like in the old days, I do vividly remember the feelings. And I am constantly monitoring my genuine emotions, as they are all muses for my writings.

The Courage to Be "Eccentric"

Creativity means *originality,* which usually means nonconformity. A recent study found that originality is essential for creativity, as long as it's accompanied by the character trait of *consolidation,* defined as the ability to put the creative ideas into motion and turn them into a book, painting, song, screenplay, clothing, or other project (McCrea 2010). It's not enough just to dream of your ideas. You've got to take action to bring about their creation.

The same study found that *neuroticism* (chronic excessive worries and anxieties) is linked to the emotional sensitivity required for a successful career in creativity. It's true! Your sensitivity is the gift that leads to inspiration, and the desire to inspire others through creativity.

If you've been teased or criticized for being "too sensitive," "neurotic," or "not normal," chances are that these cruel tauntings came from:

- Well-meaning people who were trying to "protect" you from being an outcast by pushing you to conform

- Those who weren't as sensitive or creative as you

- Those who were jealous because they suppressed their own creativity and sensitivity

Other people's opinions about you are just that: opinions. They don't define your true identity. Besides, when your creative career is in high gear, they'll take back their words. Or not. Either way, you'll know that you've taken the right path of nonconformity.

Creative people enjoy complex and novel situations. Being creative is not a hobby; it's a way of life. It means expressing your vision in all that you do and never squelching that. Live creatively!

The definition of creativity is to make something that is new. The opposite of that is conformity. Therefore, the courage to be creative means the courage to not conform.

Embrace your imagination. We've been told "You're just imagining that!" as if it's a bad thing. But imagination is the pipeline to possibility. Be open to all possibilities, noticing ideas without censoring them or worrying whether they're feasible. Don't just think outside the box . . . think like there *is* no box!

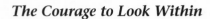

The Courage to Look Within

As a highly creative individual, you're also highly emotional. A study of 27 art collectors found that they were almost three times more intuitive and emotionally based, compared to the general population (Gridley 2004).

Those of us who have been teased or bullied internalize cruel comments and experiences, weaving them into our identity. We believe we really *are* that weird kid no one wants to play with. We expect social rejection, push people away due to insecurity, try too hard to get others to like us, and sabotage opportunities. We reason to ourselves: *Better to not even try, rather than suffer the sting of disappointment.*

How would you feel if I told you that these experiences are the *perfect foundation* for your creativity? All of those heart-wrenching experiences, every moment when you felt like a lonely weirdo, and each pang of emptiness are *ideal* starting points for your masterpiece creations.

So, the first step of creativity involves having the courage to use your own inner life as a canvas for your creations, executed using the palette of your feelings. Whatever the form of your creative project—a painting, book, song, business venture, or something else—you've got the key within your catalog of conscious and unconscious experiences and emotions.

It begins with having the courage to notice currently painful feelings, and sit with them compassionately.

This premise is based upon the fact that every painful feeling you've had is shared by countless people. If you're willing to be completely honest with yourself about those times when you feel unlovable, worthless, and like a no-good schmuck . . . and dredge those feelings to the surface . . . you can help others who feel the same way.

Popular music, books, movies, art, photography, dance, and other genres express these darker feelings, helping us recognize ourselves. Art helps us look at our shadows so they can be understood and healed. The most enduring works are those that are authentically real, coming from the artist's heart and soul.

The fearful part of our minds (often called the ego) doesn't want us to notice the shadows, because the ego controls us with unconscious fears. Once we're consciously aware of the fears, the ego loses its ability to control us. So the ego warns us that it's dangerous to look within and take an honest inventory of our feelings.

The ego tries to convince us that if we *feel* like a bad person, that means we *are* a bad person. The truth, though, is that it's the *ego* making us feel that way. In spiritual truth, we're as awesome as our Creator—because we're made in the image and likeness of our Creator.

It takes courage to look within. There's a deep-seated fear that we won't like what we find, and that all of those fears of being unlovable will be substantiated. When we hang on to secrets that we feel ashamed about, those feelings of shame are like a monster inside of us.

There's also a fear of finding nothingness when you look inside. This is especially true if you've had to adapt in your life because of an abusive upbringing or a chaotic life. *Adapting* means that you learn how to conform, cope, and get along. However, it also means that you forget who you really are, and you lose touch with your true self and honest opinions.

Looking within can feel scary, especially if you're not accustomed to it. If you're new to probing fragile feelings from an abusive past, it's a good idea to work with a compassionate and qualified therapist. Once you shine the light within yourself, you find there's a light *within* shining back at you. Instead of encountering a monster or nothingness, you find a person who's been through a lot of painful experiences, who's learned great lessons along the way, and who's been strong enough to stay alive during tumultuous events.

Once you shine the light within yourself, you find there's a light <u>within</u> shining back at you.

Having the courage to look within means that you're willing to do whatever it takes for your inspiration. Those deep, dark, raw feelings are the substance of some of the greatest paintings, songs, poems, movies, books, and other artistic creations. The reason why we resonate with these iconic creations is because they ring true. We recognize our own deep, dark places within the portrayal.

One of the most well-hidden fears is the worry that if you look within, you'll realize that you *are* crazy and unbalanced. Almost all of us highly creative types are eccentric and have been teased and ridiculed for being odd. So, the last thing you want to do is find evidence that your bullies were correct.

When we look inside, though, we find the divine spark of light. Everyone has this light, without exception. *You* have this light inside. God installed it there. You cannot be alive without the spark.

That part of you that craves helping others is the same part of you that cares about yourself. It's not a narcissistic ambition (which means thinking that you are better than others). It's also not a "guilty" caring where you think you're worse than others and undeserving yourself.

Those are all ego-based separation concerns—feeling better or worse than others, or separated from others. The caring you have for yourself is because *God* cares deeply about you, and that level of caring is inside each of your cells.

You are your own muse, your own inspiration, because you're on the inside of all of your feelings. If you look at yourself plainly and honestly—without a critic's eye and without a need for boosting up insecurities—you'll have compassion for yourself. *That's* who you want to express with your creativity

Don't cover up the painful feelings. Studies show that the best way to deal with negativity is to face it and say to it: "Look, you don't scare me one bit. In fact, you're not even real. You're just a dark cloud trying to cast a shadow over my bright inner light."

This is what happened for me when I summoned the courage to write and release my book *Don't Let Anything Dull Your Sparkle*, based upon my own journey of healing from post-traumatic stress disorder (PTSD).

All my painful experiences had compounded, one upon another, including several traumatic events. So I did research on why I was having flashbacks to a particular incident and realized that I was dealing with the effects of post-trauma. I found solid scientific studies supporting a natural approach to healing from PTSD, which I wrote about in the book.

It took courage for me to admit my experiences openly, and even more courage to release a book that wasn't in my usual genre of metaphysics and angels. Yet, writing it was a deeply personal exploration for me, and I learned as

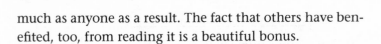

much as anyone as a result. The fact that others have benefited, too, from reading it is a beautiful bonus.

Art Connects Who <u>You</u> Are on the Inside to Who <u>Others</u> Are on the Inside

When you realize that everyone suffers from low self-esteem to some degree (well, except for narcissists, but they won't be buying your creative projects anyway, since they don't believe they need anything), then it becomes apparent that you can help others because you've been through it yourself.

Just remember this key to creative success:

- What you felt then, many other people have felt.

- What you feel now, many other people feel.

When you speak the truth about your feelings through your creations, others recognize this truth within their own selves. The wavelength energy of truth bypasses defenses and speaks directly to the heart.

The wavelength energy of truth bypasses defenses and speaks directly to the heart.

So, notice your fears and insecurities, which come in endless flavors and colors. Write, paint, sing, and dance about these feelings, as they're pipelines connecting us all. Through sharing our feelings, we allow others to feel less isolated. Like an artistic "group therapy," we see ourselves in others and think, *I'm not alone!*

Since we all feel like rejected freaks at times, you can help others by having the courage to admit it. Express these insecurities through the lens of your camera, through your beadwork jewelry, or through the soaps you create. Whatever your artistic medium, make the underlying message to the public: *I know exactly how you feel*.

You don't have to *specify* in your art that you have felt this way. It's *implied* in the art. You need to pour your heart out, but you don't need to explain why. There's no call for you to detail the events leading up to the feelings, unless you're writing an autobiography or a song. For most creative projects, it's about the feelings, not the backstory behind them.

Those who receive your art will recognize their own feelings through you. Your creativity creates a heart-to-heart connection of truth and authenticity. This opens up the hearts of everyone who resonates with your art, leaving a wake of healing.

The Courage to Bring Your Shadows into the Light

It really is about having the courage to face your feelings, including the ones that you don't feel proud of. We all have an ego, and the ego is competitive and insecure.

I can't even count the number of times I've been upset about something, and later realized that I was in my ego and acting like a willful child insisting on having my own way. The first few times that I held the mirror up to myself and saw this, I was ashamed. Now, I realize that this is a cycle we all go through. It's not *whether* we go into our temper-tantrum egotistical inner child that matters; it's what we *do* with it.

11

Hopefully, we can catch this before we do any damage to ourselves or our relationships. However, this ego energy can be channeled cathartically into creative projects. And others will recognize themselves and perhaps be healed.

There's a part of us that wants to believe that we never slip into our egos. That we're enlightened, and above fear. That desire actually comes *from* the ego, which is perfectionistic and insists that we're special.

While specialness sounds like being a prince or princess for the day, it actually leads to great angst and loneliness. Because if you're special—either specially better or specially worse than your peers—it means that you're separated from others.

The happiest place on Earth is when we realize our oneness and connectedness with others. But to get to that happy place, we sometimes have to travel through frightening shadows within ourselves.

So, these sorts of feelings—especially if they're left unexpressed—can twist themselves into emotions that may shock you when you first face them.

But then, this shock moves into compassion toward yourself and understanding. When your friends share an embarrassing secret with you, you feel closer to them. Similarly, when you face your own feelings, you feel closer to your own self. You respect how *real* you are!

Besides, studies show that when we reveal our human "flaws," other people perceive us as more likable. Psychologists call this the *pratfall*, or "blemishing," *effect* (Aronson et al. 1966).

It's about getting to know yourself at the deepest level. This is how you form a loving, trusting bond with yourself. This is how you trust and have confidence in yourself.

It's all about having the courage to be yourself.

Chapter Two

The Courage to
Feel Your Feelings

Creativity always begins with your present feelings. How are you feeling right now, for example? It doesn't have to be a traditional word for an emotion (like *happy, sad,* and so forth). It could be a metaphorical description (for instance, *untangled, piecemeal,* or *peeled*). Don't worry if the metaphor makes sense or is logical. Just start with whatever feelings you are aware of . . . and then go from there.

A big block to creative expression is the fear of publicly revealing your vulnerable feelings, as we discussed in the last chapter. Yet, each art form is autobiographical and descriptive of yourself. It's impossible to write, paint, sing, or otherwise create and not be talking about our own experience, because we view the world through the lens of our feelings and past.

Using feelings as the launching point for creativity means that you'll never feel blocked again, because you're always feeling some emotion that is a muse for your projects.

Writer's block, and similar artistic blocks, arises from trying to squeeze a thought out of your head. That means conjuring *from* within your mind, instead of allowing the idea to come *to* you.

Indeed, the amazing science-fiction author Ray Bradbury said, "I've had a sign over my typewriter for over 25 years now, which reads 'Don't think!' You must never think at the typewriter—you must *feel*. Your intellect is always buried in that feeling anyway" ("Ray Bradbury" 1974). He also remarked, "Thinking is the enemy of creativity. It's self-conscious, and anything self-conscious is lousy. You can't try to do things. You simply must do things" (Koris 1980).

Artistic block also occurs when we search outside ourselves for inspiration. We try to force a successful creative project to appear. This block stems from discounting how beautiful and inspirational our natural and normal feelings and experiences are.

When you don't recognize the treasures within your thoughts, feelings, and daily situations, you feel blocked. On the other hand, when you start with your current feelings—and face them—you then receive inspired ideas to creatively express those feelings in a way that will help others . . . and help *you* cathartically release them for self-healing.

Some people use their heads for creative inspiration, trying to figure out what will succeed in the marketplace. This approach lowers the energy vibration of the product, because it's not from the heart. Doing something commercially motivated comes from the energy of "What can I get out of my customers?" That's a *taking* energy, which is a low vibration.

Contrast that with the artist who begins with current feelings and creatively expresses them with the intention of "What can I offer my customers?" *Giving* energy is high vibrational and assures success in the marketplace.

There's an old saying about writers that I read a long time ago (and I admit that it scared the bejeebers out of me): "God gives writers [and other creative types] talent, but if we misuse this talent, it goes away."

The saying means that if writers author boilerplate books written with no inspiration, only a desire for money, God will take back their talent for writing. (Cue sound of me shuddering here.)

While I believe that God is loving and not punishing, the above statement helped me focus upon writing from my heart, not from any calculated marketing ideas. Now that being said, it's also true that in order to work full-time in creativity, you've got to have an income. Unless you're independently wealthy, you'll need a job. That's why I'm including lots of information in later chapters about how to make money while keeping your integrity as an artist.

So, this isn't a path of martyrdom, which romanticizes the starving artist. We want your creative projects to succeed, because the more people who purchase them, the more who receive the blessing of your healing intention.

The more courage you have to fully notice and express your feelings, the higher the vibration of your creation will be. Any watering down of your truth, because you're embarrassed to admit how you feel, will lower it.

Creativity and Sensitivity

As sensitive people, we feel overwhelmed a lot, without a clue about what to do with our emotions. If you've been teased for being "weird," then you're probably hesitant to reveal your underbelly to others. You already feel vulnerable enough. The last thing you want is to be told that your last bastion of privacy—your personal feelings—is wrong, too.

Sensitive artistic people can be especially prone to addictions if they're not expressing their feelings through creativity. That's because addictive substances and behaviors temporarily dull the emotional pain. Of course, the pain returns after the numbing effects wear off.

Creativity, in contrast, offers us a healthy and lasting outlet for understanding, expressing, and healing emotional pain. And we get to help others in the process, as an added reward.

There are long-held myths about highly creative people being emotionally or mentally unstable. The most prominent is that the classic artists, composers, and writers were manic-depressive or bipolar.

A simplified definition of *bipolar* is to have big mood swings. So some have theorized that, akin to manic depression, creativity involves going into the depths of despair and afterward having high energy to express the despair artistically.

In other words, the theory is that creative people get inspiration from being depressed. Then, when their mood alternates to high-energy mania, they have the motivation to paint, write, sing, or otherwise express how that depression felt. The belief is that sinking into the low emotions gives you inspiration, and when you cycle into the hyper energies, you then are able to creatively express your low points. That's when country songs about losing the love of your life are brilliantly written, for example.

There's a lot of evidence that highly creative people do go through emotional highs and lows, and there *are* studies showing that creative types are more apt to be bipolar than the general population (Janka 2004). Some artists are even labeled *manic-depressive* or *cyclothymic*, serious psychological conditions that usually require lithium or other medical intervention. Researchers find that the creative process, both in thinking style and activities, is similar to the symptoms of bipolar disorder.

However, you don't need to be manic-depressive to capitalize on this creative cycling. Most people experience a lesser extent of roller-coaster emotions and are able to function normally when they're sad or excited.

If you approach observing your "negative" emotions such as sadness, despair, guilt, shame, anger, and so on through the lens of a researcher, you'll be able to study your genuine feelings without being pulled down by them.

Be a prospector mining for diamonds among the field of your feelings. Each negative emotion is a jewel that will shine the light for others to heal.

Be a prospector mining for diamonds within the field of your feelings. Each negative emotion is a jewel that will shine the light for others to heal.

17

The Courage to Examine Your Emotions

Most of us are experts at hiding from our feelings. We know how to shut them off—or at least turn off the *awareness* of them.

There's a balance. We need to fearlessly face and express these low feelings, without allowing the feelings to lessen our drive and energy to move forward with creative projects.

So:

- Know that every feeling you have is normal and natural.

- Have the courage to face these feelings and admit them to yourself. You will diminish their strength once you do so, but the fear will be that you'll discover some "horrible secret" about yourself by facing your feelings. You won't. There are no horrible secrets about you. We all have the same insecurities, hopes, and desires.

- Have compassion toward yourself for these feelings, and know that you're doing the best you can.

- Hold the intention of helping others face and heal their own insecurities when you express yours artistically.

It's important to observe your emotions compassionately. The more appreciative you are that these feelings are part of the human experience, the more positive you'll feel—and the more productive you'll be creatively.

18

No judging

If you've been teased for being weird, then expressing your feelings publicly will make you feel vulnerable. That's normal, too, and another layer of feelings to express in your creative project. Just make sure you don't compound any negative feelings by judging yourself.

Accept that you've got natural highs and lows, and observe them objectively, with a view to expressing them in creative ways.

In my book *Don't Let Anything Dull Your Sparkle*, I cited studies documenting the importance of taking physical action to ward off stress. If we hold the stressful feelings inside, they can become frozen into chronic anxiety. Our emotions grow numb, our voice flattens to monotone, and even our facial expressions seem blank if we bottle up our strong feelings.

Action is necessary to discharge pent-up anxiety and other vulnerable feelings. For example, standing up and stretching, doing yoga, going for a walk, journaling, singing, swimming, or other activities help you to express and release your feelings.

Engaging in creativity takes the therapeutic benefits of action to a whole new level. That's because creative expression both discharges pent-up feelings *and* has the capacity to benefit others.

EXERCISE: Feeling Your Feelings

Let's say that you're feeling upset. The first step to channeling that energy into a creative work is to spend some time "visiting" with yourself:

Close your eyes, if practical, and breathe deeply.
Put your focus inside, starting with your stomach area. Don't try to label, analyze, or understand

19

anything. Just notice what you experience when you focus on the inside of your abdomen. If you sense any tension, have a conversation with your belly about why. (Don't worry if it feels silly to be talking to your body. It's still effective, even if a part of you is judging yourself for the act.)

Say or think to your belly, "Why are you tense?" Then notice any thoughts that pop into your mind. Resist the temptation to judge, ignore, or analyze your thoughts. Just notice them. Stay in your feelings, and avoid intellectualizing them.

Your body will tell you the truth about why it's tense, if you'll ask it and then be willing to hear the answer. (We sometimes block out answers we're intimidated by.)

You'll receive the answers in your mind as thoughts, words, or feelings (and no, you're not imagining them). You'll hear your belly say something like, "I'm tense because I'm bracing against stress." You'll then pick up details about what form of stress is causing your belly to tense up and brace itself.

Then go deeper in your awareness of the layers of feelings within you. Continuing on, notice the <u>emotions</u> associated with the belly tension, such as:

- *Emptiness, like there's an energy hole in your belly that you want to fill but don't know how*

- *Uneasiness or discomfort*

- *Fear or anxiety, including a fear of looking inward*

- *Defensiveness, like you're steeled for battle*

- *A sense of searching for something*

- *Shame, guilt, or embarrassment*

This is different than just trying to relax every area of your body

There are countless combinations of emotions to experience, and sometimes it feels like they're all happening simultaneously. If your emotions seem all mixed together, even knowing that is enough to extract the energy for your creative project.

If you don't seem to get any answers, that's okay. Just move on to another area, such as your heart. Interview each region of your body that seems tense or anxious. With creativity, it's important not to force anything. Stay with your authentic truth, even if that truth is "I don't know."

So in the example of interviewing your heart, first notice your current heart rate. Is it slow or fast? Labored or calm? Any sensations in your chest area?

Ask your heart, "How are you feeling?" If you immediately think of a troubling situation, interview your heart about it. You can hear your heart's truthful wisdom by asking, "How do you feel about this situation?"

In your mind, scan your body to notice any other areas of tension. Any place where your muscles are tight, use the same interview process with questions directed toward the muscles: "Why are you tense?" Notice the answers, which come to you as thoughts, feelings, words, and visions.

❋ Your intention in interviewing your tense muscles is to listen, not to fix things. At this moment, your focus doesn't need to be resolving your life situations (although you *will* hear the answers that will help you with everything, provided you're willing to take action). Instead, you're unearthing gold from the treasure chest of your feelings, because each bit of tension and every emotion is a voice calling for creative expression.

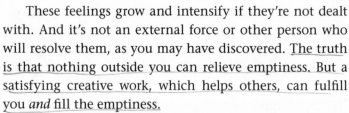

These feelings grow and intensify if they're not dealt with. And it's not an external force or other person who will resolve them, as you may have discovered. The truth is that nothing outside you can relieve emptiness. But a satisfying creative work, which helps others, can fulfill you *and* fill the emptiness.

So, having the courage to look within requires making the time and the quiet space to focus and meditate. It means not allowing yourself to be distracted by worries and fears about what you'll find. And it means having honest conversations with yourself.

The Courage to Channel Your Feelings

The creative journey has lasting and widespread therapeutic effects. As we've discussed, not only do *you* have healing breakthroughs, but you have the privilege of sharing that healing experience with others.

Remember: if you feel it, others do, too, in their own bodies. We are all pretty much the same, with universal desires for security, love, approval, and peace. We rarely have outlets to admit our feelings of vulnerability except through the arts. After all, haven't *you* heard a song that perfectly captured how you felt . . . so you listened to it a hundred times in a row?

It's the same with your creative project. Whether you're an aspiring writer, singer, jewelry maker, dancer, or other type of creative professional, you have the power to reach others through your craft. Your creative project—which doesn't even need to be "artistic" in nature—could be the therapeutic tool that helps someone else feel understood.

For example, a woman named Jay Dantzler was heartbroken after losing her son. At first, she stayed in bed with deep depression. Then she reflected that her shared passion with her son had been his peewee football games. Jay immediately began training to be a football player, and she was quickly accepted as a member of the New York Sharks.

Jay went on to become Rookie of the Year in 2007 and played professional women's football. She realized that other women could benefit from the athleticism the sport had endowed her with, so she opened up gyms called Gridiron, utilizing football training. Jay's work has been featured in *The New York Times* and sports magazines and on television . . . all because she creatively channeled her grief into a way to help others.

You're not adding to negativity by expressing negative emotions. You're actually adding to *positive* energy, because you're sending out a ray of hope for someone who feels the same. Other people will realize that they're not alone in their feelings and see that there are creative ways to deal with them.

If someone else's art has inspired and helped you, then you know what that feels like. If you haven't had that experience, then you can *create* the art you wish someone else would have made that might have healed you.

When someone comments how your creative project has touched them, you'll know those struggles were worth it. You've just helped another, which gives life meaning and purpose!

Your creative works will survive long after you've returned to heaven, so it's also a way to leave your mark on the world.

The Power of Positive Feelings

Positive feelings count, too. Lest you think that only dark emotions are muses for creativity, know that your light ones are springboards for art. After all, feelings come in every color of the rainbow.

I love the studies of intuition and creativity conducted by the Institute of HeartMath. In a review paper entitled "The Psychophysiological Basis of Creativity and Intuition: Accessing 'The Zone' of Entrepreneurship," HeartMath researcher Dana Tomasino discussed how being happy increases intuition and creativity . . . and also leads to entrepreneurial success:

> During positive emotional states, when the heart generates a harmonious, coherent pattern of activity, the resulting pattern of cardiac afferent input to the brain contributes to "cortical facilitation," whereby higher cognitive faculties are enhanced. This interaction between the heart and brain may provide a physiological basis for the growing body of evidence demonstrating a link between positive emotions and improved creativity, cognitive flexibility, innovative problem-solving, "flow," and intuition (e.g., Isen, 1998, 1999; Csikszentmihalyi, 1990; Bolte, Goschke, & Kuhl, 2003)—faculties that are also frequently enhanced during or following the generation of the psychophysiological coherence mode. We postulate, therefore, that the activation of positive emotions and the coherence mode leads to state in which higher cognitive faculties are facilitated (McCraty et al., 2006). (Tomasino 2007)

In a way, *all* feelings are positive. Using your vulnerable dark feelings for artistic inspiration means that those feelings serve beneficial purposes.

Yet, there are certain emotions that we would call more "positive" than others. That's probably because they're more enjoyable. A lot of inspirational art begins with positive feelings, such as:

- *Compassion:* When you can sense another's pain or needs. Compassion means that you respect the other person and their strengths—differing from pity, which diminishes the other person's inner strength.

- *Universal love:* There are moments during meditation when you have the realization of your oneness connection to all of life, and your heart swells with love for everyone and everything.

- *Romantic love:* If you have genuine feelings of *amore*, expressing them through creative projects will touch many other hearts.

- *Gratitude:* Creativity is a wonderful outlet for conveying your gratitude and appreciation for beauty, people, life lessons, and other experiences.

As long as it's a genuine feeling, it can be expressed through any creative medium. Think about a product or service that you would love to have, to help you feel happier. If you focus upon creating a product or service *you* desire, other people will surely desire it, too.

Attunement to Beauty

Sensitivity lends itself to an artistic nature, because you're attracted to harmonious music, beautiful art, picturesque scenery, flowing words, gorgeous fashion, and so forth. You have a discerning eye, ear, and sense of aesthetics that can be applied to your creations.

One of the reasons why I created the *Goddess Guidance Oracle Cards*, for example, is that I find femininity—in all ages, colors, and sizes—beautiful. I always envisioned goddesses as bright, ethereal examples of femininity. Too many paintings I saw of goddesses seemed dark, sinister, and jarring to my senses. So when I couldn't find a deck of appealing goddess cards, I was inspired to create my own.

This is an example of the old business success adage "Find a need and offer to fill it." If there's a creative product that you'd like to buy, and no one else has made it (or made a good enough version of it), that's your sign to create it.

When we create beauty for ourselves, it resonates at a higher level than if we're using our sales-and-marketing mind to figure out what would sell. True creativity is a gift that you give to yourself, with full faith that there's an audience out there who feels the same way you do.

True creativity is a gift that you give to yourself, with full faith that there's an audience out there who feels the same way you do.

Art as Therapy

Feelings are rarely one-dimensional. They are like ropes with lots of threads representing mixed emotions. Begin with the most prominent emotional energy, and you'll find others attached to it. As you express these energies, you give them outlets.

Art therapy is a tool in which trained art therapists help patients to express their deep-seated feelings through creativity. Usually, this involves drawing or painting, but can also include crafts, song, dance, or poetry. Studies consistently find that art therapy is effective for both adults and children in healing from physical and emotional trauma (Schouten 2015, Bar-Sela 2007, Eaton 2007).

Art therapy is particularly helpful for those who've been punished in the past for expressing themselves verbally. Through creativity, there's an avenue for venting shame, anger, frustration, hopes, and dreams.

As traumatized art therapy clients start to heal, so does their artwork reflect more happiness. Colors become brighter, the sun has a smile on its face, and flowers are blooming in their drawings.

Use your lovable, raw, hurt, angry, vulnerable, and sympathetic self as both your muse and your audience. Create a product or service to help and inspire *you*.

If you're writing a screenplay or novel, make yourself one of the characters. If you're penning a song, compose lyrics about how you feel. Write the book that you wish *you* could read. Create that crystal jewelry you've always wanted. Paint the wall mural you envision above your sofa. And so forth . . .

This is creativity from the true understanding of oneness: that as you help others, you help yourself.

Chapter Three

The Courage to Start Creating

So how do you take those raw, real feelings and channel them into a creative product or service that could support you with a full-time artistic career? There are countless ways, which fall into two general categories:

- *Create a product or service to help <u>heal or balance</u> the emotions,* such as crystal jewelry, essential oil sprays, or bath salts; soothing music, artwork, or photography; a calming new form of yoga; a book about feelings; a restorative retreat; a new modality of healing; an invigorating juice combination; and so forth.

- *Create a product to <u>reflect and acknowledge</u> the emotions,* such as a song about the feelings; a flower arrangement that evokes tenderness; a painting that captures this mood; a fiction book or screenplay centered on a character embodying the feelings; and so forth.

With art, there's no single correct mode to express yourself. Everything is a work in progress. Striving for a perfect creation is usually an exercise in frustration, and often results in the product being under continual revision. Having a desire for your creation to accurately and authentically express your feelings is a more realistic intention than trying to create a "perfect" product or service.

I find that the best way to deal with perfectionism is to start a project in the middle. There's something daunting about beginning a new project that's slightly terrifying. You're looking at a blank canvas, an empty page, uncut fabric, loose beads, or other components of your creativity. And it just seems too overwhelming, so you procrastinate until that magically elusive moment when everything's perfect and you feel prepared, qualified, and ready. That moment doesn't come around very often, and if you wait for it, your creative projects will be ignored.

Except they *can't* really be ignored, can they? That creative voice calls to you. The part of your life purpose involved with creativity awakens you with the knowledge that you need to devote time to your project. When you've been given the creative spark of an idea, it's a "conception" that grows within you, wanting to be birthed.

If you're feeling distracted, jump to the middle! When I first began writing books in the early 1980s (and this will really date me), there were no personal computers. I used a typewriter, and Wite-Out for correcting errors. So I had to type in chronological order.

When I bought my first computer in the mid-'80s and the salesperson in the store showed me how I could move paragraphs around in a document . . . it was revolutionary!

Suddenly I could write whatever topic was on my mind. I could start my books in the middle!

And it's the same with any creative project. Don't rack your brain trying to figure out how to begin. Just start with whatever you're passionate about, trusting that passion to carry you the rest of the way.

The Courage to Make Creative Decisions

Sometimes you might procrastinate expressing your feelings, awaiting inspiration for the "best" way to do so. There's a phenomenon called *existential angst,* which means getting upset because you wish you could clone yourself and take 100 different pathways at once.

Existential angst about making creative decisions (*Should I use oil or watercolor? Should this be an up-tempo song or a ballad?*) can bring up a low level of grief. It's a below-the-conscious depression, because one choice precludes another. Although there are no limits in spiritual truth, in this physical world we can't express ourselves in all ways simultaneously, like God can do.

Existential angst occurs whenever we realize that choosing one path means excluding another in that moment. For example, you can either read this book, do yoga, or watch television. You can check your social-media news feed or get creative with your artwork. You can multitask by alternating between projects, but in each present moment, people generally can only do one thing at a time.

If given a choice between two tasks . . .

- A meaningful project that seems difficult to do; or

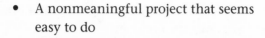

- A nonmeaningful project that seems easy to do

. . . the human mind will usually choose the easier of the two, even if it's not as meaningful.

Knowing this, you want to make your creative project as easy and pleasurable as possible. This will encourage you to spend frequent time with your project.

The ego may argue that you don't have enough money to start a creative project. That's when you get creative with your materials. Recycle, repurpose, upcycle, and use whatever you already have. Or barter with someone who has supplies you need. But don't let lack of money ever be a reason for not creating.

Be like a child and use sticks, chalk, and rocks, if need be. I know a woman who makes a great living turning old seashells into works of art and jewelry. When she runs out of shells, she drives to the beach and walks along the sand.

You can let the project speak to you as to which method it desires for its expression through you. This can put you in touch with the life force within every creative project. It has a soul, a wisdom, and an intelligence. Your creative project lives and breathes, and you are its midwife, assisting with its birth.

Each book that I write begins as a message I want to explore, and an idea I want to research, to share with others. Although I have an outline I create for every book, the specific personality of the book isn't clear until about halfway through the writing.

At that point, the book begins to *gel* with its own life-force energy. That's when the book begins to "speak" to me, and I feel it call to me with ideas it wants included in its pages (sometimes at inopportune times, like in the middle of the night!). Like a baby, the book tells me when it's hungry and what research topics it wants me to pursue.

American author and poet Henry David Thoreau described this phenomenon perfectly when he said, "Write while the heat is in you. . . . The writer who postpones the recording of his thoughts uses an iron which has cooled to burn a hole with. He cannot inflame the minds of his audience."

Like a zygote becoming an embryo and growing into a fetus and then a baby, so too is there an incubation process with our creative project. If we expect a newly conceived project to have the same life force as an older project, we'll think that there's something wrong or lacking within us. There's neither—it's just the growth cycle of any project.

Sadly, many people give up in the beginning of their artistic endeavor. Everything—whether a newly conceived baby, a newly planted seed, or a new creative project—must be nurtured until it can thrive on its own.

Although we follow the lead of the creative project's growth, we also need to stay true to ourselves and our own voice and vision.

Once you figure out what you want to express, be bold. Don't hold back, and certainly don't dilute your message. Don't overanalyze or overthink the "realness" out of your creation. Go for it!

Procrastinating your creativity by waiting until a day when you feel more confident is a mistake, because that day may never come. You're sensitive! And part of sensitivity is feeling like you don't fit in. As the late, great author Sheldon Kopp said, "I have never begun any important venture for which I felt adequately prepared."

- First you create, and then you feel ready.
- First you create, and then you know what you're doing.
- First you create, and then you realize how the project will turn out.

I have counseled many people who complained that their creative work was not as successful as they'd hoped. Almost every time, I found that the culprit was that the person was afraid to follow their vision. They watered down their initial idea because they thought it wouldn't be commercially palatable.

There's a reason why you received your original inspiration, whether it's your difficult feelings that you're working through, the urge to help others recognize and heal themselves, or a vision that was "downloaded" into your mind.

Do not veer from the vibration that is pure and truthful. Do not use your head to try to figure out what the marketplace wants. And do not tell yourself that people can't handle it or aren't ready for it. The clearer, more direct, and surer your intentions, the more widely your creative project is broadcast to reach many people who would benefit from it.

Do not veer from the vibration that is pure and truthful. Do not use your head to try to figure out what the marketplace wants. And do not tell yourself that people can't handle it or aren't ready for it.

The Courage to Dedicate a Creative Space for Yourself

Being creative requires that you be creative in making it happen. It's about being an out-of-the-box problem solver, and that includes solving the problem of "Where do I create?"

Many of us live in homes where space is at a premium, and we share it with others, so there's no extra room for arts and crafts. Don't let this be an excuse not to start creating! Instead, get creative about making a space for yourself.

The good news is that you don't need a huge room in order to be creative. It could be a corner, a cupboard, or even a drawer where only you keep your creativity supplies. Invest in an attractive portable tool chest so that you can carry your creativity supplies when you go for a drive to an inspiring location.

Besides, another benefit to creativity is that it's contagious in the most positive sense. Your creative work lifts up the energy of the place where you're creating. So, if you're involved in artistry at home, your beaming love rays shine brightly like a beacon. Energetically, those who live with you also benefit from this positive energy.

Additionally, you're a role model of expressing yourself creatively. Children watch their parents to see how to deal with stress. If they see Mom and Dad using drugs, drinking alcohol, or complaining about stress, then they will follow this example. But if they see their parents engaged in healthful stress-management activities, such as creativity, then *that's* what they will model.

A child whose parents are engaged in creative activities is more likely to try to enjoy arts-and-crafts activities at home and school. Since creativity is the heart of all successful ventures, this puts your child on the pathway to success. The child learns to experiment with creative ways of expressing themselves, so they also become a positive role model for their classmates. It's a positive creative ripple effect!

You may need to be assertive as you negotiate with family members or roommates for a space that's dedicated to your creativity. This could include a part of the dining-room table. That's where I typed my first book after my sons went to sleep at night. Even today, I use the dining-room table when I use my sewing machine. Dining tables are a great place to create while still being engaged with family activities.

When my book's royalties paid for a bigger home, I had a spare bedroom dedicated to my writing. I even utilized the floor space, where I laid out 12 manila folders, each labeled with a chapter name. Then I'd put the notes I'd written and the relevant articles I'd collected into the chapter folder associated with that topic. Once you start the process of collecting information, it synchronistically shows up and you begin noticing it because of your intention to find it. _LOA_

My current home in Maui is small, and it didn't have a room for my writing. So I hired a contractor to wall off part of the patio. _Voilà_—I had a writing room! It's tiny —only about 100 square feet. And most of the time, my Pomeranians and Sheltie pet dogs are in there with me.

But nonetheless, it's a space. And it's a room used exclusively for writing, so it's a dedicated space, which means that the energy of my little cubby office is purely about writing articles and books. When I enter the space, my whole being knows that it's time to write.

For sewing, though, I don't have such a space, which is why I use an end of our dining table. It's all about getting creative with creativity!

To the best of your ability, create quiet in your space so that you can hear, feel, and see your inner guidance. I play soft meditation music in my office to block out noise. I also get in quiet time outdoors, especially at night beneath the stars.

Your whole home should ideally be an expression of you and your creativity. If you live with others, you may need to limit creative decorating to one area of the house. But do your best to creatively express yourself where you live. Your home should reflect how colorful your imagination is! *Decorate the office space. Maybe I miss the creativity of my office. It expressed me*

Notice every thought, feeling, and impression that you have while creating. Because creativity isn't just a static decision about how to best approach a project. It's an ongoing river of emotions and ideas, and it's important to flow with that river.

Inspiration is like falling in love: it can't be controlled or even predicted, but you can set things up so that the odds are in your favor. And like love, you just *know* when it happens.

Setting up the experience includes creating that quiet space and carving out the time to receive. It usually means turning off or canceling out the noise around you. As I mentioned, I do sometimes find that soft music is calming during my inspirational receptivity meditations.

But definitely no blaring televisions, no text-message or ringtone sounds, and if your roommates or neighbors are making noise, you can wear headphones. Or take a drive out to the countryside and have an "inspiration picnic" with yourself, bringing some healthy food and a pad of paper and a pen.

Don't let noise be an excuse to avoid your creative projects. Go with the flow of whatever your environment is, and incorporate this experience into your creative expressions.

Creative Nudges

A chicken-and-egg question is whether creative ideas are generated within your feelings, and then travel outward to an idea on how to solve an issue. Or are creative ideas downloaded from the divine intelligence *as* solutions?

I believe it's a combination of both.

Good ideas will "work you" as repetitive nudges demanding to be creatively expressed. They'll call you again and again, hoping that you'll answer the call. You'll have a repetitive thought, vision, gut feeling, or some other form of inner message to take positive creative action. Do it. Take the action without delay, hesitation, or procrastination. You'll be glad you did.

Have the courage to notice the pictures in your mind, even if they make no sense or seem like fleeting images. Those mental images can be the basis for your life-changing creative project.

For example, C. S. Lewis, the author of *The Chronicles of Narnia*, said:

> All of my seven Narnia books, and my three science fiction books, began with seeing pictures in my head. At first they were not a story, just pictures. The Lion all began with a picture of a Faun carrying an umbrella and parcels in a snowy wood. This picture had been in my mind since I was about sixteen. Then one day, when I was about forty, I said to myself: "Let's try to make a story about it." (Lewis 1966)

Because C. S. Lewis had the courage to examine his mental image, and then work with this picture creatively, generations of children—and adults—have benefited from his beautiful Narnia series.

This happens to me all the time, where I'll have to stop whatever I'm doing to write a note about a repetitive idea. My office is filled with such notes, and they're always fun to explore and give expression to.

I prefer writing my ideas down rather than recording them as a voice message. The reason is that it's too easy to forget about voice messages, but if you can read the note plainly, you're more apt to act on it. You can dictate a note via voice transcription programs like Siri (on iPhones and iPads) or Dragon NaturallySpeaking software. As long as you can see what you've written, it doesn't matter whether it's handwritten, typed, or dictated.

Sometimes the repetitive messages come in the form of signs, which are things that you repeatedly hear or see with your physical senses. This happened to me when I was writing my second Hay House book, about the physiological and emotional reasons for food cravings. This was a topic I'd studied for years as an eating-disorders specialist in my psychology practice.

I knew I'd found my book's title when I heard the k.d. lang song "Constant Craving" about 40 times in the space of two weeks! I give all credit to k.d.'s song for gifting me with the title of a book to help with understanding why you might crave pizza, chips, or chocolate.

So, we return to pondering whether your creative ideas are generated by a thought, question, or experience and then expressed outwardly . . . or you have the stirrings of these feelings and creative ideas because they're sent to you by the universe, which wishes for someone to spread the word and the image.

Does the universe tap you on the shoulder and ask you to be the creator of this particular project? Or is it like a giant job board in the sky, where an assignment is etherically broadcast and whoever picks up on that vibration gets the "job"?

Either way, much of creativity involves following a path to see where it may lead you. You are following the inspiration and letting it show you the way.

Mozart is said to have written: "When I am, as it were, completely myself, entirely alone . . . or during the night when I cannot sleep; it is on such occasions that my ideas flow best and most abundantly. *Whence* and *how* they come I know not, nor can I force them" (Zaslaw 1994).

You can either allow the creative process to guide your direction as to how to best express your feelings. Or you can make a conscious decision as to which way to take your artistic project. There are always so many choices with respect to how you express the feelings and message you have. The important thing, though, is that you *start* expressing them.

Chapter Four

The Courage to Get Clarity

A lot of my creative insights and books begin with me sitting beneath the stars at night and having conversations with my feelings. Being outside frees me from energy that gets trapped within buildings. While that trapped energy might be positive, it's also *old* because it's a remnant of what I've already done. To get out of creative ruts, it's essential to go outside.

When I visited the island of Santorini in Greece in 2003, I took a lot of naps. The warm sunshine, good food, and relaxed culture made me feel sleepy. These naps were very enlightening because I'd wake up from each one with new insights, which I wrote down in a journal.

The messages I received were from a group of God's angels who identified themselves as the "Angels of Atlantis." Santorini has been long considered the last remaining landmass of the ancient civilization of Atlantis, as described by Plato in his dialogues *Timaeus* and *Critias*.

The angels relayed to me that they'd been present during the height of Atlantis and had wisdom from that time to transmit to our modern civilization.

Some of the more profound insights I received from the Angels of Atlantis were about the effect that light has on us:

- Artificial lighting is unhealthful for long periods of time.

- If you go outside and watch the sunrise, it awakens your energy, just as it encourages flowers to open.

- If you go outside and watch the sunset, it helps you sleep, just as flowers close their petals at dusk.

- If you go outside at night beneath the stars, the starlight awakens your creative energy.

When I returned home from Greece, I researched these messages and was amazed to discover how many serious diseases developed after the invention of the light-bulb. (We're talking about diseases killing millions of people annually—ones that were unknown until we all began staying indoors.) It appears that vitamin D deficiencies became rampant with the advent of artificial lighting. Regular small doses of sunlight exposure also improve cognitive functioning—our ability to focus and think (Kent 2009). I put the messages from the Angels of Atlantis into a book called *Angel Medicine* (Hay House 2004).

Since receiving these messages, I've made it a point to be outside for sunrise, sunset, and stargazing more often. I find what the Angels of Atlantis said about starlight awakening creativity to be true. On many nights, I even have conversations with the stars. In fact, the title and concept of this book came as a result of one such conversation.

StarSpiration and InStaration

Sitting under starlight while tuning in to your feelings can give you clarity, insights, and ideas about channeling your emotions into creative projects.

Scientists at Joint European Torus near Oxford, England, are working on inventions right now to harvest energy from stars, including black holes, which will be converted into an energy source for Earth. Stars are powerful!

We're all affected by natural light, and sitting outside at night allows you to bathe in that energy—without concerns about sunburn. I love when Sirius is visible, with its twinkling red, white, and blue colors.

Stars are focal points for you to look at, similar to staring at a candle flame. It's a mild form of self-hypnosis. Sit and stare at stars without any phones or other electronic instruments with you. You want to re-create the way in which our ancestors spent their evenings, prior to the invention of artificial lighting. If it's overcast, the stars are still there, and their light reaches you through clouds. If you're in a big city with limited sky visibility, the stars are still there, but they're harder to see.

One of the reasons why I quit touring was because I got depressed being in big cities where sun- and starlight are obscured by smog, light pollution, and tall buildings. I'd bring a small full-spectrum light stand with me to use during my full-day workshops (which were always held in windowless convention-center rooms).

Now that I'm home in Maui full-time with its endless skyscape, I feel so much happier and more creatively inspired. In fact, one night beneath the stars, I "heard" that this process is called *"Star*Spiration" and "In*Star*ation." The message was that our ancient ancestors would sit under the stars, and were inspired to see shapes and patterns of people and animals. They also creatively told stories about the various constellations, because their nighttimes were filled with star viewing instead of television viewing.

The Angels of Atlantis also shared with me that living on an island gives you the benefit of easily seeing both the sunrise and sunset—and it's true. While Hawaii has its issues (for example, bugs are everywhere unless you use toxic pesticides, which I don't), it's an inspiring place to write and create.

It's possible to stare at a video of stars and receive some insightful benefits. However, just as you can't get a tan without physical light, so too do you need actual starlight to reap the full benefits.

Your insights may come through other connections with nature, too. For example, going for a nature walk is a time-honored way to get clarity. Thoreau famously noted: "An early morning walk is a blessing for the whole day." His nature walks served as inspiration for his many contributions to classic American literature, including *Walden*. Modern research corroborates the link beteween natural surroundings and creativity. One study found that "interacting with nature has real, measurable benefits to creative problem-solving," increasing performance by a full 50 percent (Strayer 2012).

The exercise and fresh air help you release built-up stress, and your rhythmic steps let you process your feelings. You may find a particular place or object in nature that inspires you. It might be an old oak tree that seems to carry ancient wisdom, or a boulder that affords you a beautiful view when you sit on it. Your "muse" in nature will select you, as much as you do it.

Being a Clear Channel through Self-Honesty

The point of going outdoors to focus is to get *clarity,* which is when a realization comes into sharp focus. There's an *Aha!* sense of an epiphany. In cartoons, this experience is symbolized by a lightbulb appearing over someone's head.

Having the courage to get clarity happens when you allow yourself to acknowledge feelings that can seem uncomfortable and embarrassing, as we discussed in Chapter 2. As soon as you're *that* honest with your own self, you can feel this "click" inside. It's a sense of harmony, in which you've just brought a hidden truth to light and then let it go.

I remember struggling with finding a title for my book about time management and overcoming procrastination. The book was completed and needed a title for publication.

It got to the point where I was trying to force a title to happen. Forcing and creativity are diametrically opposed. Forcing comes from a fear of lack (of ideas, abundance, success, and so forth), while creativity comes from trusting the flow (of your honest feeling and ideas to find their audience and support you).

Forcing comes from a fear of lack, while creativity comes from trusting the flow.

Finally, it was time for the book to go to the printer. *What is the title? What is the title?* I ruminated.

Simultaneously, I was juggling raising my two sons, writing magazine articles, and other responsibilities.

What happened next is an example of the organic flow of creativity: I got so overwhelmed with the pressure of everything that I reclined on the floor just to take a time-out and breathe. I desperately wanted more breathing room in my daily schedule and fewer responsibilities to manage. Yet, making those life changes took time. And that was something I didn't seem to have enough of.

I breathed deeply and called out, "I'd change my life if I had more time!" The words hung there in the air above me, and I gasped at their naked truth.

I'd gotten clarity and found my title, in one instant of being 100 percent honest with myself about my feelings. And that's how my book *"I'd Change My Life If I Had More Time"* got its name.

I began putting the principles in the book into practice, and created the breathing room in my schedule that I'd prayed for.

My self-honesty helped me recognize feelings that I didn't even know I had. That led me to the solution. Your hidden feelings, once unlocked, can help your audience unlock their feelings as well.

For example, you may realize the role you played in an event that you had previously blamed others for. This doesn't mean you should then find fault with yourself. It means that you can now release some or all of the anger you held inside toward those you formerly blamed. What a relief that is!

Or you may discover that you're afraid to look within because you feel unlovable and unlikable. Many people do feel this way, but they don't discuss the feelings—with themselves or anyone else. They're secretly afraid that if they admit feeling unlovable, others may agree and run the other way!

So, as I mentioned earlier, imagine how much healing you can bring about by clearly exposing these hidden truths to others through your writing, painting, photography, music, dancing, and other artistic mediums. As we've discussed, there's a huge sense of relief when we realize that we're not alone in our feelings. *You* and your creative projects can be who and what bring about this relief.

You mine for these hidden truths within your own soul, because your soul *is* your true self and also the pipeline to the Source, to God, to the divine. Inside of you is a telephone hotline to direct-dial heaven, and you can funnel all of that comforting communication through your creativity.

This is the higher purpose of your artistic inspirations. This is why you were born to create. Like the sun continuously emitting rays of light, so too are you meant to constantly express creativity through your projects.

Striving for Clarity of Expression

Clarity also means having the courage not to tiptoe around what you want to say. That way, the message won't get lost or confused. Be direct, with no extra words and no apologies—just your unvarnished expression of your truth. This gives others the courage to express their truths, too.

An adage I've lived and worked by is "Write to express, not to impress." That means being very clear about what you're trying to say, and then saying it clearly.

Sometimes insecure writers hide behind big words and jargon that no one can understand. Or if the *writer* doesn't really understand what they're writing about, their writing won't be understandable. In New Age circles, some spiritual teachers and authors use terminology like *ascension*, *seventh ray*, and other esoteric phrases. These terms sound lovely, but if your audience can't understand what you mean in concrete, practical terms, they won't relate to you. And if they don't relate to you, they'll move on to a teacher they *can* relate to.

A study I conducted in college showed that <u>people remember words if they can visualize them</u>. For example, if I say "cat," you know what I mean because you can envision a feline animal. But if I say "cosmic consciousness," it won't be understandable or memorable.

Speak, write, and otherwise express yourself in down-to-earth ways, even when you're talking about unearthly topics. If you're unsure about this, imagine having a conversation with a seven-year-old, and explain the concept to this child in a comprehendible manner.

The Courage to "Mine" Your Feelings and Get to the Heart of the Matter

One thing's for sure: As you express your feelings creatively, you get more clarity about them. Each creative project is like strapping on a miner's hat with a headlamp and venturing into a mine shaft. You can only see the step that you are on right now, and there's uncertainty as to what you are mining.

Remember that the creative process isn't necessarily about solving or fixing a problem. That can happen as a side effect. What it's really about is peeling away the layers of emotions to get to the heart of the matter.

In truth, when you deep-dive into observing your true feelings, your life improves. That's because unconscious fears, once exposed to awareness, can never control you from the shadows again.

When you start any creative project, there's never a guarantee that it will be satisfying, commercially viable, or successful. But you do it anyway, because the creative spark wishes to be expressed.

You begin your mining, layer by layer, with little more than hope and faith, until you recognize a glimmer of gold beneath the colorless rocks you've been picking at. With continued faith, and the willingness to work, the shining gold starts to be more apparent and visible.

This is the courage to trust the flow, allow for ambiguity (but strive for clarity), and be creative.

Chapter Five

The Courage to Listen to Divine Inspiration

Many of our favorite songs, books, movies, and other creative projects were divinely inspired. The person was just sitting there and—*boom!*—an idea came to them. They followed through with action to turn the idea into reality, and they were successful.

We can recognize the vibration of divine inspiration when we hear, see, or read it. There's a clear energy of truth, which we instantly recognize in our gut.

When I played guitar in a band called Obsidian, our keyboard player, Mark Watson, wrote gorgeous original songs. (You can watch us playing together with a You-Tube search of "Doreen Virtue Obsidian.") Mark told me that he'd hear these songs in his head, often as he was awakening.

Similarly, Kerry Livgren said that he wrote "Carry On Wayward Son" for his famous band Kansas when the whole song popped into his head like it was "beamed down." The song was an answered prayer for Livgren, who's deeply spiritual and now a devout Christian.

At that time, Kansas was under pressure from CBS record producer Don Kirshner to produce a hit song. Their previous three albums had been critical but not commercial successes. Kirshner said that he and the studio were losing money on the band. The threat hung over them to get a hit or be dropped from the label.

Kansas had been recording their fourth album, and they only had three or four songs prepared. So, each night Kerry Livgren would pray, listen, and "hear" a new song, which he'd then present to the band members in the morning at the studio.

The album was finally complete, but no songs with "hit" potential had emerged. It was at that point that Livgren recalls that the words and music for "Carry On Wayward Son" were downloaded into his head. He took them into the studio the next morning, and Kansas finally had their hit song, which saved their musical career.

Sometimes when your back's against the wall, you make a fervent prayer and surrender your ego. You're humbled, because what you've been doing hasn't been working. So you get out of God's way and open yourself up to divine inspiration.

Another artist, Akiane Kramarik, began drawing at age four when she says God spoke to her and encouraged her to paint and draw. Akiane's mother and father were both atheists at the time, so she had no parental influences directing her toward divine communication. As a self-taught prodigy, she had no formal art training, either.

Akiane has now created thousands of paintings portraying her visions of heaven and the world, many of which now hang in galleries around the world, and her art commands thousands of dollars. She's also appeared on major television shows because she's so inspirational.

(Take a moment to do an Internet search of Akiane's work for a heart-opening experience . . . By the way, Akiane's artwork inspired her parents, too, and they are no longer atheists. They now believe in God and Jesus, thanks to their daughter's paintings of our Lord.)

Divine Assignments

I put myself through college and paid my bills by working as a secretary at insurance companies. Aside from my nice co-workers, it really was horrible work. Each day, I'd take dictation by putting on headphones and listening to one of the insurance claims adjusters describe an accident or robbery. I'd type every word they said onto insurance claims forms. Listening to and transcribing all these negative experiences put fear and negativity into my mind daily.

But even the most painful and unpleasant experiences can help us learn and grow. In this case, I learned how to type up to 100 words per minute—mostly so I could get through my work quickly.

It's just another example of how every experience delivers valuable lessons and skills. From that dreadful secretarial job, I learned to type superfast. So now with my work as a writer, I can type as fast as I think . . . and as fast as I receive divine inspiration.

As you may know, most of my books and card decks are about God and the angels. I've connected with angels since I was a little girl. I was born highly sensitive to energy, including picking up on what others are feeling. And, as I mentioned at the beginning of the book, much of my childhood I felt alone and misunderstood. It didn't help that the other kids teased me for being weird and "too sensitive."

So I retreated a lot, spending time with my two beloved pets, Mickey (a big long-haired orange cat) and Corkey (a fluffy Himalayan). With the cats, I felt accepted and loved.

And then there were the angels. I was raised Christian, but our family's emphasis was on God and Jesus. We never discussed archangels or guardian angels. Everything was about the Gospels and our Lord.

So when angels would visit me during my loneliest moments, I didn't know what to think. Their loving, benevolent energy would calm and soothe me.

While I worshipped only God and Jesus, I continued communing with the angels as I grew into adulthood. Angels brought me comfort and profound messages that helped me personally (like guiding and supporting me to give up wine, coffee, animal products, and anything with chemicals or pesticides in it). Their presence was always gentle and welcome . . . and still is.

So it's not surprising that I turned to angels for help with my writing. At first, my books and articles were on topics related to my psychological work. I wrote about recovering from eating disorders and also about relationships.

But as much as I loved writing, my heart wasn't fully into this type of subject matter. I could hear my angels guiding me to write about spiritual topics. However, I resisted their guidance for fear of what others might think. The memory of children teasing me for being weird made me rationalize that my psychological writing was helping people.

Yet, the angels showed me how empty I felt when I saw my printed magazine articles about relationships.

Although I was grateful to be published, I didn't feel fulfilled. *"That's because this type of writing is not your purpose,"* they'd whisper to me. Still, I had no idea how to write about spirituality, as they were guiding me to do.

I later realized that when God gives us a purpose and divine assignment, the angels whisper the details about how to fulfill that assignment. We receive these messages in our heart as feelings, in our head as ideas and know-ingness, or in our mind's eye as visions and dreams. The angels, after all, are messengers of God, so they know the best way to guide us.

How do we know if it's a real and trustworthy messenger of God, and not something else disguised as an angel? The Bible says, "By their fruits you shall know them" (Matt. 7:20), meaning that true angels never speak about egoic effects of what you can "get" (like getting rich or famous, for example).

The angels speak only about the service you can *give* to others, using your natural talents and interests. If in doubt as to whether an idea is divinely inspired or not, ask God to send you a clear sign. Know that angels of God are entirely safe, loving, gentle, and trustworthy.

If you're unfamiliar with working with angels, here are a few basic guidelines:

- Angels respect our freewill choices. They don't intervene unless asked. It doesn't matter *how* we ask (thinking, praying, affirming, writing, singing, visualizing, or otherwise). All that matters is that we *do*.

- The angels are God's messengers, and extensions of our Creator. We can speak directly to God or the angels. They are one.

- We don't worship angels. The only worship goes to God. Angels are gifts, protectors, guides, and companions to us from God.

- The angels help everyone who asks. Offering unconditional love, they are entirely forgiving and nonjudgmental.

- Angels are nondenominational, so we don't need to earn their help or belong to a certain religion or subscribe to any ideology to call upon them.

- Angels are different from departed loved ones, who can act *like* angels but who still have human egos. True angels are pure egoless light, love, and intelligence from God's mind.

- Everyone has guardian angels with them at all times. The key is to keep our minds sober and quiet so that we can hear our angels' messages from God to keep us safe and on the right path.

- Angels are pure divine energy, without physical bodies. Therefore, they don't have a gender or race. However, they can take on temporary human form in order to help and protect. ("Be not forgetful to entertain strangers: for thereby some have entertained angels unawares" [Hebrews 13:2] is a quote by Saint Paul describing this phenomenon.)

- Because angels are pure energy, they can never get tired. They are also omnipresent, like God, so they can help many people simultaneously.

- The angels' lack of ego means that they would never judge you, nor would they become angry or frustrated with you. Angels are purely unconditionally loving.

The angels can't violate God's will or your free will, so they walk a fine line when you ask them to assist you. They're not Santa Claus, delivering every wish on your list. However, they can help you be your very best, and that includes creatively.

One of the ways in which the angels have helped my creative process is by teaching me how to calm and focus my mind. I receive their messages, like most of us do, as strong feelings and impressions. Those gut feelings to do the right thing, walk your talk, and live in integrity come from our higher self and the angels.

If we ignore those feelings, the angels will speak more loudly through signs (repetitive messages that we hear or see with our physical senses). And sometimes, we'll hear an actual voice guiding us to safety and health.

Ever since I almost lost my life in 1995 when I ignored the divine warnings (an event I'll describe in the next chapter), I've done my best to listen to the angels' messages. So when the angels guided me to stop drinking caffeine and wine so that my mind would be clear and focused, I did.

In fact, I asked God and the angels to help me avoid withdrawal symptoms, and they miraculously did! I cold-turkey quit drinking coffee and had no headaches or cravings. Same with wine. The angels will help anyone who asks them.

In retrospect, I realized that caffeine had caused 99 percent of the anxieties I'd previously had, fears that prevented me from doing my best creative work. Caffeine also triggers nervousness that can erode your self-confidence as an artist. If you suffer from performance anxiety, stay away from caffeine, sugar, and other stimulants that cause jitteriness.

Now I drink chamomile tea as my hot morning beverage, and I'm more efficient with work than ever. I found that being relaxed is optimal for creativity, not get-up-and-go caffeine.

Detoxing from alcohol had similar benefits, in that I no longer had hangovers and foggy thinking in the mornings. I suddenly had more productive hours in my day! And that extended into the night, as well. In the past, I wasn't able to write once I had my evening glass of wine. So I'd lose several hours of prime writing time while "relaxing" with alcohol.

The greatest support for my detox came through prayer. Keep praying for heavenly help, and it is given. In fact, studies show that spirituality and religion are beneficial for healing from addictions (Walton-Moss et al. 2013). Alcoholics Anonymous and other 12-step support groups are also founded upon the spiritual principle of surrendering to a higher power during recovery.

(These 12-step support groups for healing from addictions can be found in cities worldwide, as well as through free online meetings. You can find them with an Internet search for "12-step meeting.")

The Angels of Creativity

In addition to the *guardian angels,* who are with every one of us (whether or not we believe in angels), *archangels* watch over us all as well.

These archangels are unlimited and egoless, tireless beings who simultaneously assist everyone, having unique individual experiences with each person. Their purpose is to help manage the guardian angels and bring about God's will of peace for all.

The ego may say, "But I don't want to bother or exhaust the angels!" This is simply because fear energy doesn't want love energy to be in charge.

Always remember that God is unlimited, and so are the angels created by God. The angels don't have physical bodies, so they can't get tired. They are fueled by pure divine love. They also care about each person equally, so they help everyone who asks.

We don't pray to or worship the angels, but we do appreciate them as the messenger gifts God deemed we needed (and whom we do need for peace, guidance, and protection).

Archangels for Artistry

Each archangel has a different specialty, which relates to the help they give us with creativity. The archangels assist us with anything that increases peace among people and on Earth. They know that creative projects are beneficial for promoting inner peace. So it's the archangels' sacred honor to lend you a hand with any creative project that will bring blessings to the planet.

Here are the archangels to call upon for creativity assistance. We aren't praying to the angels, nor are we worshipping them. We are merely invoking our freewill choice to receive divine support for our life purpose.

— **Archangel Michael** is the famous angel whose name means "He who is like God." And just like God and all the angels, Michael is unlimited, egoless, and tireless. Michael's specialties and purpose include releasing us from our egos and the grips of fear. Michael is the angel to call upon whenever you feel insecure about your creative abilities.

You don't need a special prayer or invocation to elicit Michael's support, and you don't need to be a religious (or even a nice) person. It's not about earning his help—because Michael is enacting God's will of helping everyone to be at peace and live at their highest potential. Michael helps everyone, because he is God's right-hand angel for restoring us all to peacefulness.

Just thinking, saying, writing, or singing Michael's name is enough to call upon him. And then pour out your heart with whatever it is you need help with. Tell Michael about your insecurities, worries, and fears.

Michael will listen without judgment, and then wield his sword of light to disentangle you from fears that are blocking your creativity. Gently and swiftly, he will dispel your insecurities and lend you strength, confidence, and motivation to complete your creative project. He'll also give you the courage to market and sell your creative services and products (more on this topic in Part II).

When you call upon Archangel Michael for the first time, you may wonder if he hears you. He does. His very presence will make you feel warm with his flaming sword of light, and some people begin to perspire when Michael is near. You'll suddenly feel more courageous, with clear, grounded thinking.

— **Archangel Gabriel** is the famous Annunciation angel from the Christmas story in the biblical book of Luke, who says to Mother Mary, "Behold, I bring you good tidings of great joy!"

Gabriel was the only angel who spoke words in the Bible, always delivering important messages from God. Gabriel spoke to the prophet Daniel, to Abraham, to Saint Anne, and of course to Mary.

Gabriel's name means "the strength of God." However, most people think of Gabriel as the "messenger angel" with the trumpet, heralding vital news. Gabriel also assists human messengers who are relaying information that could help humanity.

Archangel Gabriel helps creative messengers, including writers, teachers, singers, actors, screenwriters, songwriters, musicians, and those working with any other uplifting art form. In my book *The Miracles of Archangel Gabriel*, I included chapters of true stories of people who became successful in their creative fields with the help of Archangel Gabriel. These stories involve authors, screenplay writers, actors, and so forth who received work in their respective creative careers.

As with Archangel Michael, you don't need to earn or elicit Gabriel's aid. All of God's archangels are ready to step in, as long as you've made a freewill choice to ask for help and as long as it's God's will for you.

Think, speak, or write the name *Archangel Gabriel*, and this amazing angel is with you. As mentioned before, the archangels are unlimited and can be with everyone simultaneously, so you needn't worry that you're pulling Gabriel away from someone else.

It's not blasphemous to call upon an angel. However, if your beliefs entail that you should talk directly only to God or Jesus, it's important to honor them. You can always ask God to send Gabriel to you, and it will be done.

Sometimes people tell me they have difficulty believing that an angel described in the ancient Bible could still be with us. When you call upon Gabriel to help you, you'll know that this remarkable archangel definitely *is* around in modern times!

I've personally experienced Archangel Gabriel being supportive of creativity in the following ways:

- *Motivation:* When you don't feel like working on your creative project, Gabriel will gently but firmly nudge you into action—sometimes, guiding you all the way until it's completed. I give Gabriel credit for my prolific writings, because the angel is like an encouraging coach who says, "Keep going—you can do it!"

- *Inspiration:* Archangel Gabriel can help you overcome blocks and be able to more clearly receive divine inspiration.

- *Reaching an audience:* I've seen Gabriel act like a manager or an agent, helping human messengers get their creative works published and seen by the public.

Of course, you don't *need* angels to receive divine creative inspiration, which is available directly from God's mind to yours. I find that angels are like supportive and caring co-workers who keep me on track with my writing and other creative projects. They can even help you to know *Is this project really a good idea or just a distraction?* so that you won't waste time on the wrong path.

Messages from the Angels about Creativity

We all receive messages from God, our higher self, and our guardian angels through our intuitive feelings, epiphany thoughts, dreams and visions, and signs from above.

The question isn't whether we're receiving this input . . . it's whether we *listen* to it.

Someone once asked me why, if I really hear angels, I have been divorced. The answer I gave is that there's a big difference between *hearing* the angels and *listening* to them:

- With hearing, you get the message. You're aware that your angels are guiding you to, for example, improve your diet.

- With listening, you actually *do* something about it.

When I got married (and even before), I definitely heard my angels cautioning me not to do it. I also noticed the red-flag warnings that my partner wasn't appropriate. But being the raised-on-fairy-tales romantic that I am, I overrode the messages.

Looking back, I can see that I was both willful and also in a romantic fog, imagining that things would get better after marriage. I didn't listen, got married, and ended up divorced. The angels were right. They always are. Now I do my best to listen to them and put their guidance into action without hesitation or delay.

Here are the messages I've learned from the angels about creativity:

1. Break any project down into little increments. Instead of being overwhelmed by the enormity of the project, focus on *What can I do right now?* and then do it. From the angels I similarly learned: *Write a page a day, and in a year you'll have a book.*

Most of my books aren't written over long periods of time. This should be reassuring to anyone who believes they need endless days of free time in order to create. Rather, I will sit and write for an hour, then get up and do something else, and return to my desk for an hour more of writing.

When I was touring to offer workshops, and also when my sons were young, I'd have even less time for writing. I'd be lucky to get 15 minutes per day. But that's enough, if you approach creativity with consistency.

In fact, a number of studies find that it's best to get interrupted while you're creating. I know it sounds counterintuitive, but researchers have found that "being interrupted to work on an unrelated task increases solution rates for creativity-related problems" (Sawyer 2012). The interruptions trigger new ideas that you can then apply to your creative project.

So, for example, if your child interrupts you to ask a question about her homework, this will ultimately help your child *and* spark new ideas for your creative project. The trick is that you *do* return to it after you're done helping with the homework.

However, I do find it important to stop whatever I'm doing to write down those fleeting "butterflies" of inspirational ideas. So I'll make a little note, putting it right next to my laptop so I won't forget about it, and then my mind is free to deal with any interruptions to my creative project. When an epiphany comes into your mind, be sure to jot it down before it flutters away back into the ether.

2. Have faith that there's a purpose for your creativity. Even if you have no idea what you're doing with your creative project, or whether it's commercially viable, have faith. I've followed my guidance many times to work on creative projects that—while they themselves didn't culminate in a business profit—helped me in nonmaterial ways such as having fun, learning new skills, fulfilling a dream, enjoying a novel experience, gaining confidence, and so on.

I'm a firm believer that everything in life can be our teacher if we're open to learning its lessons. And each job we hold teaches us new skills that can be used in our creative work. That being said, though, if you want to make creativity your full-time job, it's important (especially in the beginning of your creative career) to make every minute count.

3. Know that it's okay to express your vulnerability publicly. People can relate to you more when you're real and authentic, which includes being open about your natural emotional reactions. Your creative project resonates deeply with people who recognize their own vulnerable emotions in the way you've creatively expressed yours. You can heal other people's shame and low self-esteem when you help them recognize that they're not alone in how they feel.

4. Think only thoughts of love and success, and that's what you'll attract. I received this message from the angels many years ago, and I didn't believe it at first. But I wrote the sentence on a big piece of paper and taped it on my office wall. I read and meditated upon the message, and put my focus on thoughts of love and success. Whenever I'd nose-dive into fear, I'd pray for help to focus on the positive . . . and my thoughts would return to being peaceful.

Learning not to judge is hard . . . remember the cube

5. Use fragrance, sound, and lighting to lift up your energy. The angels told me that fragrance (essential oils or flowers), sound (particularly soft music), and lighting are bridges between the physical and nonphysical worlds. They said that if you have beautiful sensory stimuli around you, it lifts your creativity up to heaven. Your artistic projects become higher-vibrating. I began applying this tip when I wrote *The Lightworker's Way*, and I found that it set a peaceful tone for my writing. I've been using fragrance, sound, and lighting as inspiration ever since.

The Courage to Partner with Jesus

I was raised Christian, with a love and admiration for Jesus, and I also have a personal relationship with him, as many do and as anyone can. I've come to know Jesus as a way-shower of strength, compassion, and wisdom.

I don't see Jesus as a source of fear or guilt, as some religions unfortunately emphasize, but as a source of strength, forgiveness, compassion, and love. As a Christian, I look to him as my Lord and Savior. But I've also come to recognize that Jesus is nondenominational and loves everyone.

For writing and also for giving speeches, I call upon Jesus because he's the most incredible wordsmith I've ever found! When I'm at a loss for words or unsure how to represent a feeling through language, Jesus always comes through. His words arise as thoughts and a voice that I hear. He chooses just the right phrasing to convey esoteric and profound concepts. Jesus is the teacher of teachers!

Prayers for Creativity

I believe that there's no single correct way to pray. Spirituality and religion are deeply personal choices. Here I'm including the prayers that I often say, and I encourage you to be spiritually creative and add whatever is in your heart. Make each prayer an in-the-moment, genuine, and sincere conversation with your Creator.

A Prayer for Inspiration

I say a prayer like this whenever I feel uninspired or blocked:

> Dear Lord,
> Please help me open my heart to this project, and find my way to loving it and expressing love to and through it. Thank You for filling my mind with inspiration and guiding me to express my true feelings and thoughts.

use these as a source for intentions

A Prayer for Motivation

This is a prayer that I say when I feel distracted:

> Dear Lord,
> Please help me keep my focus upon my creative work, use my time wisely, and devote myself to completing this project with joy and with dedication to it and the people who will enjoy it.

A Prayer for Letting Go

I say this prayer whenever I feel myself getting into my willful ego and need to return to the will of the divine:

> *Dear Lord,*
> *Thank You for helping me to keep surrendering the need to control the direction of this project, and instead trusting your divine will. I know that I am not the owner or the initiator of this project, but that I'm a conduit carrying it to completion. I focus only upon following the divine direction that You give for each aspect of the project.*

The Courage to Work with Unicorns

Most people are accepting of angels, since they appear in many cultures and the iconography of various religions. Well, how do you feel about *unicorns*? They're an interesting part of my creative journey, too.

Like many children, I was obsessed with horses. I collected little horse models, read books about horses, and got a job on a Shetland-pony ranch mucking stalls (shoveling horse doo-doo) in exchange for riding privileges. I loved unicorns, too, but my main focus was on horses.

Then I began giving angel readings to clients, and I clairvoyantly *saw* unicorns with several of them! These weren't imagination. The unicorns were just as real as the angels and saints I saw with my clients.

When I visit art museums, I'm always pleased to see how many old paintings include images of unicorns. They're iconic symbols—or perhaps these artworks show a tragically extinct animal who once roamed the earth and was perhaps hunted to extinction for its horn. Regardless, there's a reason why unicorns have been revered for so long.

The pattern I found was that those who had unicorns as their spirit guides were always highly creative people. The unicorns were there to help them express their high-vibrational ideas and have the courage to be unique and ahead of their time.

In my readings, I also saw unicorn spirit guides with highly sensitive children (those whom I refer to as "Crystal Children"), a sign that these youngsters were very pure and needed to retain their childlike awe and imagination. The unicorns also indicated that the children would benefit from regularly engaging in arts and crafts.

Having unicorn symbols in your creativity space will boost your courage, imagination, and purity of motivation. The unicorns guide you to focus on your true passion, without regard for what others may think. They clear the path for divine creativity to travel from the Source, through you, and into your project.

So I highly recommend investing in a unicorn statue or two, as well as posting some unicorn artwork around your creativity space. (In most of my oracle-card decks, you'll find at least one unicorn painting . . . to purify and uplift the energy of the deck and to connect with those who understand unicorn energy.)

In a way, the courage to be creative means becoming like a unicorn in which *you* are magical, rare, unique, and original. So *be* a unicorn . . . and have the courage to create!

Chapter Six

The Courage to Quiet Your Mind and Be Receptive

When people ask me for help in learning how to hear divine guidance from God and the angels, it's really a request for them to learn how to be *receptive*.

Creativity is identical. It's the courage to listen. It's the courage to feel, hear, think, and see truths that may trigger temporarily unpleasant emotions and realizations. It's the courage to look at yourself and receive inspiration.

Why would we be afraid to receive inspiration? Well, our higher self isn't afraid at all. But the ego certainly is. The ego rules with fear and its offshoots of doubt, worry, and anxiety, knowing that if you go straight to the Source of inspiration, it will no longer be in charge. You will be receptive to *love* instead of fear.

So the ego tries to con you into staying stuck in fear, and its main method is to convince you that you are safer if you remain hypervigilant and afraid. The ego wants you to endlessly scan for potential concerns and problems, in a misguided attempt to control them.

Your higher self, which is your true self, has nothing to do with fear or worries, but instead stands quietly receptive, bathed in the rays of love and light God continuously broadcasts everywhere, to everyone.

Receiving inspiration is never painful or fear based, but it can *seem* so as you act like that miner digging through beds of rock to get to the gold and gems in your interior.

The courage to be receptive is about releasing control to the benevolent universe, which is one with your higher self. It means that fear won't be in charge; *love* will.

The Courage to Listen

Receptivity begins the moment you hold the intention to listen. This is an individual-personality decision. I'm sure you've met people who are really good at talking, but not so good at listening. Perhaps you've been that way yourself.

Very often, these are the same people who tell me that they can't hear God. I have to gently ask them to stop *talking* to God long enough that they can *hear* God's answers.

The reason why someone engages in a barrage of chatter is because they're afraid of silence. It's like the philosopher Blaise Pascal's well-known quote from his *Pensées*: "All of humanity's problems stem from man's inability to sit quietly in a room alone."

The fear of silence is really the fear of being alone with yourself. It's the fear that you won't like what you find when you "sit quietly." It's a fear of boredom, because the traumatized self has learned to crave danger and excitement from years of harsh experiences.

So the traumatized self will seek out and create drama to satisfy its need for excitement. This is a topic I wrote about extensively in *Don't Let Anything Dull Your Sparkle*. With creativity there's a quieter form of excitement—not from experiencing problems, but from *solving* them.

During dangerous situations like near car accidents, we can become temporarily receptive because we surrender to the fact that we don't know how to handle what's going on. It's like the old aphorism "There are no atheists in foxholes," referring to the fact that soldiers without any spirituality will turn to prayer when they fear for their mortal lives.

Similarly, when people are in an overwhelmingly frightening situation, they frequently receive divine messages, which—if followed—will save their lives.

This happened to me during a carjacking attempt in 1995. I had willfully ignored guidance that told me to put the top up on my convertible or the car would be stolen. But later, at the moment I did find myself with two armed men demanding my car keys, I had no choice but to surrender to hearing the message from God's angels.

After years of selectively listening to divine guidance when it fit my own desires and was convenient, or when I felt competent enough to trust the guidance, I was humbled that day and finally became receptive. I'm alive today because of it.

I pray that you don't have a brush with death in order to pop open your receptivity. There are gentler ways to become receptive. As I mentioned before, it all starts with your decision.

Exercise: Receptivity

I would advise that you view receptivity as an experiment. Just like scientists test hypotheses before either accepting or rejecting them, hold the intention of trying out receptivity to see if it improves your life and adds to your happiness or not.

1. Decide that you're ready to be receptive.

2. Create opportunities to receive. This means that you'll need to carve out at least 30 minutes of uninterrupted quiet time. It could be while you're falling asleep or when you're first waking up or in the shower.

3. When you receive inspiration, immediately write down or record the inspiration. As I've discussed, inspiration and creative ideas are like butterflies swooping through your mind. If you don't metaphorically take a photo of that butterfly, or write about it, or even capture it right then and there, it will keep flying away.

I believe that there are ascended masters who know what ideas are needed in this world, and they broadcast those ideas widely, waiting for one to be plucked from the ether by anybody who has the courage to make it into a physical reality. Those same masters will help you each step of the way, but you have to be the first to take action by writing down the idea.

So let's say that you've decided to be receptive and you're in a place of quiet, with your cell phone turned off and no distractions or interruptions. The next step is to relax.

It's easy to get performance anxiety with your own self, feeling pressured to get that great idea. It requires patience. The moment you are relaxed, even if your mind is wandering, is when ideas come to you.

For me, I best relax under the night sky. Sitting beneath the twinkling stars, even on cloudy nights when I can see only one or two, helps me feel connected to the gigantic universe and its inspiration, support, and messages. The messages we receive when we're outside in nature are gentle and kind, so there's nothing to fear or be intimidated about.

Focus on listening to both the voice of the universe—the voice of the infinite wisdom of God—and your own inner voice.

In a way, it's a conversation between your higher self and the divine wisdom. Yes, in spiritual truth, you are one with God and the universe. And it's also true that you presently live in a 3-D physical world of duality. This is the world that you paint, sew, sing, create, and write in.

Receptivity makes creativity easy. Once again, it's a matter of noticing your feelings and thoughts, without judging or stopping them.

The Flow of Giving and Receiving

You are receptive whenever you completely let down your guard and enjoy the present moment. You are receptive when you allow yourself to be cared for and loved. You are receptive each time you allow yourself to receive.

Both giving and receiving are equally important, and they are natural aspects of the physical world and life. Breath in, breath out. Tide in, tide out. Changing seasons, the cycle of day to night. They're all aspects of giving and receiving.

The practice of tithing is similar, in which you give 10 percent or more of your income to an organization or needy person that spiritually inspires you. You don't make this donation in order to receive, but it always happens that way. What you give is blessed tenfold, and you always receive exponentially more.

A woman called my radio show and complained that she only had $2 to her name. I guided her to donate one of the dollars to whomever she felt guided to give it to.

When I spoke with her years later, she explained that she gave that dollar to a homeless person. She said that the next day, her abundance started to flow in. She got ideas for a business, and felt confident enough to go for it. Today, she is financially secure and, even more important, she is happy. Giving is always followed by receiving.

We don't give in order to receive, because that would be giving with strings attached. Instead, we give from the pure joy of giving . . . and the universe gives back to us joyfully as well.

I loved a speech that I saw country singer Reba McEntire make after winning a music award based upon her fans' votes. She thanked her fans by saying, "I've always tried to play a game with you guys, with the fans, to try to out-give you. I've never won." In other words, the more you give to your art, the more you receive.

The Courage to Surrender to the Creative Flow

You already have experience with being receptive each time you watch a movie or read a book where you let go of logic and allow yourself to enter the story. You drop your defenses and enjoy "believing." There's a wise saying among writers: "Write what you know." What this means is to write (or paint, speak, or otherwise create) based on your own experiences.

You don't need to research another culture, because your own culture will be interesting to someone else. You don't need to reinvent something—you just need to tell your own story. There's a therapeutic benefit to sharing your story. It's cathartic.

Others will naturally resonate with your story. The law of attraction automatically ensures that those who benefit from your art form are drawn to it and will find it. (Of course, you still have to do some marketing of your art, which we will discuss in Part II.)

So, receptiveness isn't necessarily about receiving some-thing profoundly different from what you've already felt and thought. It's more about getting clarity on the truths of your life. Just because the creative inspiration seems familiar to you, don't discount it. Others aren't familiar with your domain, so it will be a revelation to them.

Receptivity will also guide you as to how to begin and continue a project. You'll receive impressions with your physical and spiritual senses—for instance, as thoughts and ideas, as if God has downloaded a file into your mind with all of the complete knowingness, or as a feeling and a hunch. Perhaps you might even receive a vision of the finished product.

Everyone is different with respect to how they receive, and your experiences with your mode of receptivity can change according to the project and what's going on with you. The point is to be open to receiving inspiration in many different ways. If you expect inspiration to come as a lightning-bolt idea and it arrives as a subtle feeling instead, it's still equally valuable.

If you expect inspiration to come as a lightning-bolt idea and it arrives as a subtle feeling instead, it's still equally valuable.

Why are enthusiasm and optimism for a creative project frequently followed by dashed hopes and discouragement? Because there's a belief in instant gratification. Too often, artists will give up because their project isn't immediately turning out the way they'd imagined, or because of a delay in selling it.

Find joy in the process of creativity, not just the end result (sales, for example). This puts higher energy (love energy) into your work and attracts wonderful opportunities, great people . . . and success.

Creativity means surrendering to the will of your higher self and God. Instead of "deciding" how a project will go, you follow guidance step-by-step in the moment. It means listening carefully in each moment, and responding to the direction that God and the project are taking you.

When I begin writing a new book, I approach it like a secretary taking dictation. The secretary listens to, and faithfully types, each word as it's given. For the first 100 pages or so, I have no idea what the final book will be like. I'm simply typing with full faith that the book will make sense to me later. Until then, I'm merely a typist bringing through information with my typing fingers.

It's the same way with any form of creativity. Whether you're designing a dress, painting a mural, choreographing a new dance, or creating a new recipe, let go of trying to steer the direction the project goes in. Surrender the need to control the outcome, and enjoy the ride it takes you on.

Quieting Your Mind

You'll receive more creative inspiration by taking the time to quiet your mind. If life seems too busy and noisy for meditation, this will take some effort and dedication on your part. And it's *so* worth it!

Just a little time devoted to quiet listening, and you'll be tuned in to the inner creativity coach that's always available to help you. The divine wisdom will come through for free, 24 hours a day, with trustworthy guidance.

A recent study found that meditating for 30 minutes a day heightened creativity, especially emotion-based creativity, as we're discussing and describing in this book (Ding et al. 2014). The researchers concluded that creativity isn't something that's inherent in a select few individuals, but is a skill that can be developed through healthful habits such as meditating.

Researchers concluded that creativity isn't something that's inherent in a select few individuals, but is a skill that can be developed through healthful habits such as meditating.

79

If you've never meditated before, please don't let the word *meditation* intimidate you. Like creativity, meditation isn't the province of an elite or exclusive club. While the word itself may conjure visions of agile yogis sitting in lotus position, that's only one form it can take.

The true definition of meditation is quieting the mind enough to listen—to your honest feelings (even the ones that are intimidating), to your thoughts, and to the divinely inspired answers you are receiving from God.

With practice, the mind stops chasing after answers. Meditation allows it to be a peaceful observer and participant, filled with blissful faith that *all* needs are provided for. There is no lack, no time urgency, no competition. Just an enjoyment of the present moment.

To begin a new meditation practice, set aside ten minutes daily at a consistent time. Early morning is best, because it sets a positive and peaceful tone for the day. However, evening meditation is also helpful in resolving anything that bothered you that day.

If ten minutes are difficult to come by, five will do. It's not the quantity but the quality of time that matters. There's no "right" or "wrong" way to meditate. Any form of mind-quieting and heart-opening is healthful to you and beneficial to your creativity.

There are many different meditation processes. You can sit, stand, walk, or lie down. Your intentions may vary in each instance, such as:

- *Relaxation meditation:* Holding the intention of relaxing the muscles in your body, and letting go of any mental, emotional, or physical stress. Soothing music can be a helpful accompaniment to this form of meditation.

- *Problem-solving meditation:* Entering your meditation with the intention of receiving solutions. You may not sense an immediate answer, but this form of meditation gets the wheels turning so that one will come when you're ready to receive it.

- *Prayerful reverence meditation:* Meditating while thinking about God or your beloved ascended master (Jesus or Buddha, for example). One method is to send love from your heart to theirs, and then feel the magnified healing love bounce back to you.

- *Mindful awareness meditation:* Closing your eyes, breathing, and noticing. Objectively observing your thoughts, feelings, and other processes. Not judging yourself. Just compassionately observing.

- *Creative meditation:* The form of meditation I do when I'm creating a new deck of oracle cards. I'll look at the image for each card while sitting in meditation with my eyes open in a soft-focus gaze. I breathe and stay open to God and the angels speaking to me through the artwork so that I receive a message, which I then put on that card.

- *Releasing meditation:* Holding the intention of letting go of anything that's unbalanced, unhealthful, or toxic. With each exhale, intend to release lower vibrations and afterward inhale higher vibrations.

- *Healing meditation:* Focusing upon balancing and restoring your physical body. This can include visualization of illness or injury being lifted away, enveloped in healing light, and so forth.

- *Heart-opening meditation:* Thinking of everyone and everything for which you are grateful. This is a wonderful meditation to prepare you for a new relationship or to heal an existing one.

A meditative state can also occur when you're involved in a repetitive activity, such as gardening, swimming, running, sewing, and so on. Thoreau engaged in meditation as he walked through the natural surroundings of his home near Walden Pond, Massachusetts.

Anytime you're in a trance, you can receive divine messages. This can include while you're watching television, which relaxes and opens you up to energy (one more reason to be discerning about the programs and commercials you watch).

When I was around 19 years old, I was watching a mindless television program one night when suddenly I had a vision and received a divine message. In my mind's eye, I saw myself and a big silver trash can. Then I saw the trash can grow larger and come toward me like a giant metallic flexible straw. It was if the trash can was going to consume me. I then heard a voice say: *"You're throwing your life away."*

Poof! The voice and vision were gone! Shaken, I intuitively knew the meaning of the message. I'd been spending too much time "slacking," where I lazed around; ate junk food; drank alcohol; and wasn't doing anything to improve my life, help others, or grow. That was a wake-up call that inspired me to follow my inner guidance and return to college.

Although it's uncomfortable to receive confrontational divine messages, they can also inspire us to move forward and launch us on a creative path.

In a way, all forms of meditation are creative. After all, meditation connects us to our divine Creator, the Source of all creativity. Meditation moves us away from focusing upon time and earthly concerns. We become aware of how we truthfully feel and of the guidance from our guardian angels.

Chapter Seven

The Courage to Make Time for Your Creativity

Let's face it—our lives are busier than ever. With technology, it seems we spend hours surfing the Web, texting, and e-mailing. We have hectic family and personal lives, plus our career to attend to.

If you have a full-time job to pay the bills, how are you supposed to have enough time for creativity?

The answer is through *multitasking*. This means that you work on your creative project while also fulfilling your other responsibilities and self-care routines. For example, you can do research for your creative project by watching a documentary while jogging on the treadmill, or you can pair a visit to an art gallery with a girlfriend get-together lunch.

Studies show that successful creative people tend to multitask and work on several creative projects simultaneously. One study concluded that the projects cross-fertilize each other, with ideas sparked from one helping the others (Gruber and Davis 1988).

If you get bored easily, or if your creative interests are varied, then work on two or three projects simultaneously. This of course goes against sage advice counseling you to specialize and focus on one thing at a time. Certainly, that's what my former literary agent advised me to do. While I love my ex-agent, I'm a bigger fan of how Reid Tracy, the president of Hay House, has given me free rein to write as many books and card decks as I want.

I have so many messages coming in from our sacred Creator and the angels that I have to type as fast as I can each day to keep up. I'm usually working on four books and two or three card decks simultaneously. While this sounds frantic, it really is a way of channeling creative energy in a constant flow.

Creative Multitasking

The creative process of working on several artistic projects opens you up in a big way. Energetically, it's the creative equivalent of being a gymnast or a yoga teacher, because you become so limber, flexible, and open to new ideas. The more time you spend with your creativity, the more the ideas flow like a huge river moving through you.

You have two choices when the creative ideas are flowing: try to control them or swim with them. I choose the latter.

Besides, if you're someone with a short·attention span, multitasking is the best solution. If you're working on Creative Project A and reach a point where you're bored or uninspired, you can immediately jump over to Creative Project B, and so forth.

With practice, multitasking becomes easier and more natural. You learn how to create in five-minute intervals. You become okay with getting interrupted by your kids or an appointment. You adapt to creating in short bursts, and little chunks of time. In fact, you learn to become highly creative with time management!

Napping

You can also sleep or nap while working on your creative project. In fact, many famous inventions and creations were produced this way. Beethoven received inspiration during his naps, as did the surrealist artist Salvador Dalí.

I love the story of musical legend Paul McCartney having a dream about his departed mother, whose name was Mary. She had passed away when he was 14 years old. During a time when the Beatles were experiencing strife among the band members, Paul had been drinking and partying excessively. He also worried that he was alone and single, while the other Beatles all had committed relationships.

One night while Paul was sleeping, his mother appeared to him and said the words "Let it be." Paul knew instantly that this was a sign to let go of the stress, and be at peace with the unfolding of events. He then put this message into song lyrics, in which he says that in troubled times, Mother Mary comes to him. So "Let It Be" was born of a dream visitation.

Naps increase our right-brain creative activity, according to Georgetown University neurology professor Dr. Andrei Medvedev (Gardner 2013). One interesting study found that people who napped were twice as likely to be able to solve a problem involving a video game right after they awoke, compared to those who didn't nap (Bei-jamini 2014).

Dreaming

Researchers have concluded that interpreting your dreams can also give you more creativity. In a 2002 paper, researcher C. A. Alfonso wrote: ". . . the process of dream interpretation may . . . motivate artists to more freely create works of art." (I deleted the psychology jargon from his sentence for clarity.)

You can interpret your dreams in a *dream journal*, which is a notebook you keep on your nightstand with a pen. First thing in the morning, write down or draw whatever fragments of the dream you remember. With practice, you'll recall more of your dreams.

If you argue that you don't dream, it means that you're not aware of your dreams or can't remember them. Everyone dreams, because having rapid eye movement sleep is physiologically necessary. You can learn how to remember your dreams with five minutes of journaling each morning.

Creative "Marinating"

Studies also show that someone who views a problem first and then walks away from it to think about it arrives at more creative solutions than do those who force themselves to struggle for a solution.

So a creativity principle is to take time to let the situation marinate in your mind for a while. Go distract yourself or take a nap, and let your unconscious mind work on the solution. But don't walk away for too long, as there's a difference between taking time to think about solutions and procrastination.

Healthy Productivity

There are many creative people who've never put their ideas into action because they lack the energy and motivation. As I mentioned earlier, creativity is to some degree linked to bipolar disorder (also known as *manic depression*) and a lesser version, cyclothymia. Inspiration and depth are plumbed from depression, and the manic phase is when you put those ideas into action. Mania gives the person confidence, energy, and happiness, which are correlates of creative action.

Medical intervention and lithium treatment are usually necessary for manic depression. There is some promising research, though, about natural treatment of bipolar or manic-depressive conditions. These include having a consistent sleep schedule, exercising regularly (especially with yoga), getting daily doses of full-spectrum sunlight, having a healthful diet, detoxing from alcohol and caffeine, and meditating (Uebelacker 2014, Soreca 2014, Ives-Delipeir 2013, Jacka 2011, Benedetti 2001, Maremmani 2011).

Amazingly, these are all the steps that *I* was intuitively guided to take, and I can attest that they work—even though I never suffered from bipolar or manic-depressive conditions. A healthful lifestyle has given me the ability to multitask without getting distracted.

With that said, don't make "getting a healthier lifestyle" a reason to procrastinate working on your creative projects. The following healthful lifestyle characteristics will definitely even out the roller-coaster highs and lows (thus giving you more inner peace, happiness, *and* consistent energy that can be devoted to your creativity):

- A positive and optimistic outlook

- Healthful eating

- Regular exercise, especially yoga

- Consistent sleep hours

- Consistent full-spectrum sunlight

- Detoxing from chemicals

However, I find the action that gives me the greatest peace and happiness is <u>devoting daily time to creativity.</u> <u>It's that connectedness with Source, and "exercising" the</u> <u>higher self, that makes creativity as necessary and pleasur-</u> <u>able as breathing.</u>

The Courage to Take Charge of Your Schedule

"Giving away time" means that you are putting your own needs last in your schedule. Probably the biggest part of being your own authority figure (a topic we'll cover in Chapter 16) is taking charge of your schedule:

- If you feel that you don't have enough time for creativity, then you are giving away time.

- If you feel frustrated because there's never enough time for yourself, then you are giving away time.

- If you feel guilty for relaxing or taking time out for creativity, then you have given away time.

Who owns your schedule? *You* do. Unless you're a minor, in the military, or a prisoner, you have the right to choose how to spend your day. Yes, there are responsibilities, and consequences for doing things like skipping work or school. Yes, if you have dependents, then their safety and needs are factors in your schedule. But the bottom line is that you have the choice.

You already know that each day, you are given 24 whole hours, like a time-bank account that is continually replenished. Those hours belong to *you*. Like everyone, you've got a few "musts" that call to you, like eating, tending to children, cleaning, working, and so forth. As long as you realize that *you* are in charge of deciding how you spend your time, you'll feel empowered. You are choosing to cook dinner for the family, instead of complaining that you have to. You are deciding to clean the house, instead of feeling sorry for yourself. These are take-charge attitudes that superpower your energy and give you authority over your schedule.

Contrast that positive energy with someone who feels victimized and complains that she "has to" clean the house. Do you feel the disempowerment of blaming others for her schedule—like she's being controlled as a victim?

Feel the difference? See why it's essential to be in charge of your schedule?

Of course you have responsibilities to others. We all do. But the point isn't whether there are responsibilities or not. It's that you realize you are *choosing* to spend your time on them. You do have a choice, always.

That's the starting point for getting control over your schedule. Just like it's important to balance and manage your finances, so it is with balancing and managing the hours in your day.

An Hour a Day

You can fritter away your money by buying lots of inexpensive things. Similarly, doing lots of little activities can chew up the hours in your day.

To take charge of your schedule, you'll need to save at least one full hour of your day that you will devote to your creative pursuits. If you put an hour a day toward creativity, your projects will take on form and come to life very quickly.

It doesn't take an eternity to create a masterful work that will inspire and help others. But it does take a commitment to putting in steady amounts of time.

When I decided to write my first book, I had a full schedule caretaking for my two young sons. I also worked as a secretary and went to college part-time. How would I find time to write?

My solution was to write for one hour after my sons went to sleep. I made it a nonoptional nightly practice. Many a night, I wrote instead of accepting party or movie invitations. My priority was to keep my promise to myself to write an hour a day, no matter what. And look what happened: I've now written dozens of books!

Very few of us have the luxury of hours of free time. Most of us are juggling responsibilities, which give us—if we're lucky and very careful with our schedule—one or two free hours a day.

You can even create in *less* than an hour a day. Keeping a notebook handy (including a notebook app on your mobile phone or tablet) is a way for you to record your creative ideas while you're on the go. Sometimes I only spend ten minutes writing. As the angels reminded me, if you write a page a day, in under a year you'll have written a book.

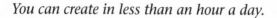

You can create in less than an hour a day.

The point is to do something daily related to creativity. It's exactly like keeping your body's muscles toned through regular exercise. By focusing on creative ideas and expression daily, you promote a fountain of new ideas coming to you.

Make time for breaks and self-care, too. Henry David Thoreau credited his nature walks with clearing his mind and inspiring his writing work. This is especially true if you feel your stress levels rising during the creative process. Get up and walk away, but be sure to come back to your creativity.

Time Journal

Early in my writing career, I took a college class where we were assigned to keep a "time journal." The teacher wanted to show us how we were utilizing—or squandering—the hours in each day.

Like a food journal—in which you record everything you eat, and then are amazed by how many calories you're consuming—my time journal was an eye-opener for me. In a notebook, I logged every activity and how much time was involved.

At the end of the first day, I could see the pattern in the ways in which I was using time. I saw the hours spent in front of the television, watching shows I didn't really care about. I saw how my long girlfriend gab-fests on the telephone cut into time I could spend with my children, on self-care, and on writing. Clearly, I needed to find balance.

There's nothing wrong with allocating time for enjoyable leisure activities. Devoting the whole day to productivity is a formula for misery and health issues. But if you're engaged in activities that are neither productive nor enjoyable, you've got to ask yourself, *Why am I doing this?*

That journal taught me to reserve shorter amounts of time for activities like talks on the phone or television viewing. Looking upon activities as a buffet, in which you can take a little of this and a little of that, helped my schedule "plate" from growing overly full. I felt much better and lost the victim-martyr resentment of feeling like I didn't have enough "me" time.

Be creative and challenge yourself to see how much extra time you can create by letting go of inconsequential activities. If you can, for example, cut down on reading your social-media news feed, you'll have extra minutes (or even hours!) that can be dedicated to your creative project.

Filling out a creativity schedule is helpful. Make creativity appointments daily, and keep those appointments with yourself.

Deadlines

Most of us are inspired by deadlines, and once you get a publishing contract or an art contract, you'll have due dates from your publisher, manufacturer, or distributor to deliver your product. Before then, it's helpful to make your own deadlines.

When I got my first book publishing contract, I was ecstatically happy. But then I felt overwhelmed when I realized that I had a deadline to finish the book. It seemed like a huge responsibility, one that rested squarely on my own shoulders. No one was going to write this book for me. I had to do it on my own.

Soon after, I bought a tea mug that said "If it's going to be, it's up to me," to inspire me to take responsibility for my actions. This focal point really helped me mature in my outlook, too. I became more accountable about how I'd spend my time. I didn't procrastinate or get distracted as much. And on my spiritual path, my motto is "If it's going to be, it's up to *We*," meaning our partnership with our Creator.

The first thing I did to keep myself accountable was to buy a monthly wall calendar with big daily squares. On each of the squares, I wrote a self-imposed writing deadline. For example, I gave myself two weeks to complete each chapter. So, I wrote in ink—so I wouldn't erase the commitment—"Chapter 1 due," "Chapter 2 due," and so on, every two weeks.

Then I made a pact with myself to complete a certain amount of writing daily, such as 1,000 words, or four pages (a typed double-spaced page is generally 250 words). I made this a nonoptional activity, in the same category as brushing my teeth and hair.

I recommend you do the same, if you respond well to deadlines. The key is to turn whatever commitments you make about your creativity into must-dos. They are not in the category of *Well, if I have extra time, I'll get around to it*. Treat them as you would an important appointment, because that's what they are!

It's not that we can force creativity to happen on the clock. It's more about being *prepared* when opportunity strikes. I find that if I'm at my laptop keyboard, I'm more apt to be inspired to write than if I'm away from my computer.

However, you can capture those inspirational ideas by carrying a notebook or using the Notes app on your mobile device. It doesn't matter *how* you notate those beautiful butterflies of divinely inspired creative ideas—just be sure to do so . . . so that they don't fly away, out of your conscious awareness.

With that said, don't go "chasing" the butterflies of creative ideas. You're a satellite-dish receiver, not a butterfly net. In other words, sit quietly and the butterflies (the ideas and inspiration) will come to you.

Keeping your promises to yourself, such as upholding your commitment to create daily, helps you form a stronger bond with yourself. We all trust people who act in trustworthy ways. That includes acting honorably toward yourself.

In writing this book, for example, there have been days when I used all of my assertiveness training to say no to invitations that would have distracted me from writing. Yes, I would have enjoyed those activities also. But I wouldn't have fully enjoyed them if I was longing to spend time on my creative project, this book.

Ray Bradbury, the prolific science-fiction writer, told an interviewer: "I discovered very early on that if you wanted a thing, you went for it—and you got it. Most people never go anywhere, or want anything—so they never get anything" ("Ray Bradbury" 1974).

In other words, books get written when you sit there and write them. As much as I love my guardian angels, they don't magically write my books while I sleep. I'm the one who has to sit at the keyboard and type. It's the same with any creative project. It only gets done when you log the hours and work on it.

A creative project is a relationship that you commit to nurturing. When you take time away from the creative project, it's important to be honest with yourself about the reasons, such as:

- A must-do responsibility (like feeding and caring for yourself and your young children)

- A choice that you give yourself permission to fully enjoy (like spending time with friends or family)

- An unconscious decision to procrastinate working on the creative project because of perfectionistic fears about the project

- Allowing yourself to be distracted from your priorities by others' priorities

- Saying no to distractions, which sometimes involves rescheduling with people who are asking for your time

Speaking of using your time wisely, let's explore that topic next.

Chapter Eight

The Courage to Stay Focused

Doesn't it seem like there are a multitude of things vying for our attention, now more than ever before? Perhaps it's social media, or maybe the intention of going faster and doing better. Collectively, these factors exert an "attention deficit" effect upon us.

Creative expression requires time and focus, as it's a form of meditation. Yet, how do you block out distractions? What if you have children, pets, a business, or dependent people who need your constant care?

I understand. When I began writing, my sons were very young. They're grown now, but they still need their mother's love and attention, as do the many pets who live with me. In addition, there are friendships to maintain, income to produce, a home to keep clean, food to prepare and eat, and health and fitness routines.

As we discussed in the last chapter, it's up to you to take charge of your schedule and safeguard at least one hour a day for your creative priorities. During that time, though, how do you stay focused and not become distracted? Let's discuss this important topic.

Dealing with Distractions

As I mentioned in the beginning of this book, when given the choice between two tasks, one a high-priority but more difficult task and the other a low-priority but easier task, it's human nature to choose the easier task.

Your creative work is your priority, but it can seem more difficult. The stakes are higher, because you are counting on the creative project to open new doors in your life. So, it's easy to justify distractions as a way of "preparing" you for your creative work.

For example, you may be distracted by social media and e-mail, and rationalize that you need to build your platform and networking contacts to support your creative work. Yes, it's true that these days, artists need large social-network followings. However, if that social network distracts you from being an artist in the first place, what's the point?

Most distractions are "delay tactics," which the ego uses to steer us off the path of our priorities and life purpose. Examples of delay tactics include anything that's time-consuming such as addictions, drama-filled relationships, perfectionistic housekeeping, and endless research.

We know it's a delay tactic when we defensively justify the activity as absolutely, vitally necessary to do instead of our priority task. No one can tell us otherwise, even though we know deep inside that it's pulling us away from better choices.

So, the first step in avoiding distractions is to practice rigorous self-honesty. Observe how you avoid working on your creative projects, and honestly face the reasons why:

- If it's a fear of being ridiculed, then know that every person who creates does receive some criticism. It's not *if* you receive criticism, but what you do with it that matters. (This is a topic we'll delve into further in Chapter 10.)

- If it's a fear that your dream won't come true, then know that it *will* come true if you keep working on it. The way in which dreams come true is usually different from our expectations, but we do ultimately have control over *whether* they materialize. It's all about devoting continual daily time and effort to the dream.

- If it's a fear of being inconvenienced by the amount of time required for creative work, then know that, yes, you'll need to make choices about how to spend your time. Is going to the shopping mall really more important to you than working on your art? It's a choice. You're either going to say yes to your creativity or yes to distractions.

- If it's a fear of being pressured to keep up your creative work, then know that this pressure only comes from within. If you want to create one masterpiece and then hang up your creativity hat, you have that right. But most likely, you'll enjoy the process so much (even the stressful parts) that you'll want to continue creating. Some creations will be your best work, while others will reflect a more relaxed you.

- If it's a fear of missing out on fun, then make sure your creative work *is* fun.

These are just a few examples of fears underlying creativity that could cause you to look for distractions so that you have a perfect excuse not to work on your projects, I've done this. We've all done this. Still, being distracted is neither fun nor fulfilling. It's a time-waster, unless you learn and grow from the experience.

"Virtual" Distractions

If e-mails, phone calls, and social media are distracting you, then you'll need to turn off the Internet or the devices. You may worry that you need your telephone to be continuously on "just in case" there's an emergency call.

What I've learned is that the more creative we allow ourselves to be, the more intuitive we also become. With this intuition, we're always connected to our loved ones. In Hawaii, we call this the "Coconut Wireless," meaning that our loved ones can pull on our energy if there's an emergency and we'll feel it.

In the meantime, it's healthy for you and your family members to have some space so that they can figure out things on their own . . . especially if you've been playing the role of the responsible one who fixes and takes charge of everything. Let your loved ones grow by fulfilling this role for themselves. Don't worry—you'll still be needed.

You may feel a sense of withdrawal at the thought of unplugging from e-mail, phones, and social media. That's because we can get addicted to the brain chemical and stress-hormone highs of being constantly online. There's a rush and an excitement associated with the constant novelty of virtually connecting.

That's why it's doubly important that your creative projects make you so excited and filled with happiness that you would rather work on them than do anything else. The moment your creative project feels boring, you can be sure that your audience will be bored also.

Pour genuine excitement, joy, and passion in your project, and this is what will inspire your audience to become passionate about your work. Your feelings, poured into the work, elicit those positive feelings within others.

But what if you're pouring darker feelings—such as sadness, loneliness, despair—into the work because that's how you genuinely feel? As long as you are feeling emotionally satisfied by the project, you will inspire your audience as well.

Because it's not always the sugary-sweet projects that open a person's heart. Think of a tragic book, movie, or play that has moved you, as an example.

The more your creative work is a natural extension of your interests, the more time you'll willingly devote to it. The more your creative work feels therapeutic to you, the more you'll look forward to working on it.

If you find yourself distracted—or looking for excuses *not* to work on it—this is a sign that you're off the course of your true feelings. Get back on track, and make the project an authentic and honest reflection of your inner truth. It's the only way to stay enthused about, and committed to, your creativity.

Sometimes the ego will distract us with side projects that seem related to our true creativity but which are ultimately diversions that keep us from our path. The ego constantly tries to justify taking actions *other* than our creative project: *I just need to check my e-mails . . .* and *I want to see who posted on my Facebook page . . .* and other wandering thoughts.

Fortunately, even those diversions have benefits when they lead to insights. For example, I can write about these distractions and help you through them because I've experienced them myself. In the same way, as you watch how your ego intrudes on your creativity, you can understand yourself better. This allows you to help others through the same process with your creative works.

Procrastination and Perfectionism

Procrastination is another word for *perfectionism*. The inner critic—perhaps modeled after some adult in your past who seemed to criticize you—wants everything to be perfect before you dive into your creative project. Since perfection doesn't exist on Earth, this means perpetually delaying your creative work.

Salvador Dalí (who was expelled from the art school he'd attended) said, "Have no fear of perfection; you'll never reach it." In other words, perfection is unattainable, so don't waste time and energy trying to achieve it. Of course, if you're building an airplane or something that affects human safety, you'll want to construct it carefully. But perfection is impossible in art, books, movies, food, and other creative endeavors, because everyone's opinions about what is perfect are different.

Sometimes, procrastination involves using "delay tactics," as we discussed earlier. *First my house must be spotless, and then I'll be allowed to work on my creative project.* See the perfectionism in this sort of delay tactic?

This perfectionism carries over into the fear that you aren't capable of creating the perfect project. The fear is that it will be deeply flawed and you, and others, will be disappointed—or worse. These fears make it easier not to even begin the project.

Boredom

We often get distracted because of boredom. We're just not into it, so we look around for something exciting or entertaining.

If there's any part of the project boring you, that's a signal to cut it. If it bores you, it will bore others. You're an artist who *inspires* others. You might relax them, but you don't want to make them yawn.

So if you find yourself avoiding a certain part of the creative project, question why it's there. Could someone else do that part? For example, framing the painting you made. Or is the avoided part even necessary?

Remember that creativity is about expressing your unlimited divine nature with infinite possibilities. Just because it's never been done before, doesn't mean that it *can't* be. Just because there's a normal and conventional way to do things, doesn't mean *your* project needs to be normal or conventional.

Work on only what ignites your passion and excitement. It may require diligence and patience, but it's a labor of love. ♡

Financial Insecurity

You may also have times when you feel insecure about moving forward without having a guarantee that this will work. *Is it a waste of time, energy, and resources?* you may worry. This is especially true if you've quit a secure job, or are considering doing so.

Most of us need to earn money to pay our bills and purchase supplies. You don't want to depend on your creative work to be the source of your income, though. It's best to work part-time at an income-producing job so that you don't have to put pressure on your creative work to support you. Remember, if you're creating just to make money, this intention lowers the energy of your project . . . and repels potential customers.

Approaching creativity just for income, or with underlying fears about making money, muddies the project with low-vibrational energies. We will discuss overcoming fears about earning a living through creativity in Part II.

Battling Blocks

If you find yourself blocked or distracted while you're sitting at your creative work space, sometimes it's helpful to get up and move. The act of gentle exercise and stretching can change your brain chemistry so that you release stress and feel more inspired.

When I was writing my novel, *Solomon's Angels*, I felt anxious because it was my first fiction book and it involved so much cultural and historical research. Instead of sitting in front of my computer, trying to conjure a story line, I took a day off and booked a seat on a snorkeling boat. As I sat on the boat, with the wind blowing while I stared at the ocean, I received the inspiration that I needed.

As if I were watching a movie, I saw the opening scenes of the book and got a sense of the direction for my writing. Usually, I carry a little paper notebook or use an electronic one on my phone. But on the boat, I had neither, so I allowed the scenes to play out in my mind, and knew that I'd remember them just like after watching a powerful movie.

From that moment on, I didn't experience any writer's block with *Solomon's Angels*. It was an enjoyable experience, just as other novelists have described, where the characters took on a life of their own and led the story line. I didn't want the book to end, and I still think of the Queen of Sheba and King Solomon as dear friends.

So, getting up and stretching or going into nature is a way to inspire yourself to create. Just make sure that your path leads you back to the place *where* you create.

Focused Meditation

It's so easy, when you're creating, to let your mind wander. That's actually a form of meditation and channeling.

Letting go of your surroundings and retreating into the inner world of timelessness *is* a way to be present with your project, so long as you continue to work on it physically. Dreaming about the project won't get it done, unfortunately. It really is a case of "If it's going to be, it's up to me."

On the one hand, you've got to let go of thoughts about the material world so that you can access high-vibrational energies and ideas. And on the other hand, it's about being grounded enough and present enough so that you can translate all of those energies into something physical (a book, painting, song, or what have you).

Creativity is a form of focused meditation. This means that you have an *intention* while meditating, as opposed to free-form meditating, where you open up to whatever comes to you. With focused meditation, you act as

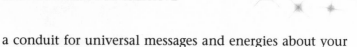

a conduit for universal messages and energies about your creative project.

Imagine the top of your head having a satellite-dish receiver, which is tuned in to high-vibrational, loving, pure channels of energy. You collect those energies and distribute them into your mind, emotions, and body. They're then concentrated and are funneled through your hands into your creative project.

A lot of times during focused meditation, out of the blue I'll receive a book title like a thought that's downloaded into my mind. I had this happen with several of my titles, including *Angels 101, Goddess Guidance Oracle Cards*, and this book.

With *Angels 101*, it was like I was seeing the words in front of me, as clearly as I'd see a physical sign, and I relayed them to my publisher, Reid Tracy, the CEO of Hay House. He immediately understood that it was important for me to write this book about the basics of guardian angels and archangels, and he said yes without a book proposal. (In the U.S., the term *101* refers to an introductory college class, like Psychology 101, History 101, and so on. I understand that the title has been changed to *The ABC's of Angels* in some parts of the world where "101" isn't a common expression.)

Detoxing to Increase Focus

The ego wants to raise doubts continually, because it is fear based. So, the ego will pepper you with questions such as *Will people like this?* and *Will this sell?* It reminds me of an anxious child in the family car constantly asking, "Are we there yet?"

Your higher self, in contrast to the ego, enjoys the journey. One of the ways to stay focused within your higher self is to detox from anything feeding the ego's anxieties and fears,

If you're highly sensitive to energies and emotions, you're likely also highly sensitive to chemicals. When I seriously committed to my writing career, I had to detox from a daily habit of drinking strong coffee and wine.

I used to drink the wine at night to sleep, because I was wired from downing so much coffee during the day. Then I had to drink more coffee in the morning because I was hungover from the wine I'd consumed the night before.

Prayer and meditation helped me to break this cycle and, as I mentioned before, to detox without headaches or withdrawal symptoms. Sometimes, though, it's wise to work with a recovery professional to guide you through the process safely.

Once I detoxed from wine and coffee, my mind cooperated and was able to focus. It reminded me of the ability to steer a car straight down the street, as opposed to driving while intoxicated or having nervous hands.

In addition, my manifestation efforts (visualizations, affirmations, positive thinking, and so forth) became more focused, like a laser beam, thanks to my chemical-free mind. I realized that I'd previously been like a driver "under the influence" with my visualizations, veering into the negative lanes and in and out of positive thinking. No wonder my manifestations had been feast-or-famine!

Once I detoxed, I could keep my focus squarely upon my goals and intentions. No more swerving into doubts. I haven't craved coffee or alcohol at all since, especially not with all these newfound benefits.

(If you'd like to detox, there's plenty of free support available through 12-step programs, like Alcoholics Anonymous. You can even find effective 12-step groups with online meetings.)

Focusing on Intrinsic Rewards

If you find yourself avoiding your creative project, spend time meditating on *why*. Is it a fear? Perfectionism? Or does something need to be changed with the project? Resistance to creating has an underlying cause that is trying to communicate with you. Listen to that message, and you'll revive your motivation and enthusiasm for your project.

Like a heart-to-heart, honest discussion with a loved one, you need to listen to the reasons why you don't feel like creating today. Having this conversation with yourself will help you fall back in love with creativity and lose those fears triggering procrastination and deliberate distractions.

This is one more reason why it's important to choose a creative project that you sincerely resonate with. Ideally, it will be enjoyable. If you enjoy the project, you will naturally look for ways to spend time working on it. You will steal moments from your schedule so that you can commune with the beautiful energy of your beloved project.

Contrast that experience with someone who uses his head to logically figure out what the marketplace wants (a trap we talked about in Chapter 2). If he doesn't really believe in the project, and isn't excited about it, his focus will be on whether the project makes money or not.

We call this external focus *extrinsic*. Studies show that when people expect to be rewarded for their creativity (with money, praise, promotions, good grades, or other outside incentives), their creativity decreases. Researchers believe this is because they have their eye on the prize, instead of focusing on their inner feelings and inspiration (Sawyer 2012).

And if you aren't emotionally invested in the project, it's easy for you to walk away, as opposed to someone who *needs* the project for their soul, like a desert nomad needs water.

Intrinsic rewards mean that you get joy and pleasure from the creative process. There's ecstatic relief as you get these feelings out and express them creatively, whether you're singing soulful lyrics, painting the colors of your emotions, creating healing crystal jewelry, writing a cathartic journal entry, or engaging in any other form of creative expression.

Intrinsic rewards are the most satisfying and lasting of paths to happiness. It's pure bliss to take time from your busy schedule and responsibilities and devote it to an artistic endeavor. There's a high that comes from having faith that you're guided in each moment of the project.

The Courage to Notice Delay Tactics

As I've been talking about throughout this chapter, we get distracted from creating because of fears, including the fear that the project won't be perfect. So we create delay tactics in the form of diversions that we engage in because we're unconsciously trying to keep ourselves busy instead of working on our creative project.

For example, after I sold my first book to a publisher, I faced the daunting task of writing it. The pressure I felt to

write a wonderful book, and to have it completed by the deadline, was stressful.

So I'd unconsciously look for ways to not write, to avoid these uncomfortable feelings. For instance, I'd notice that the carpet needed vacuuming. I'd vacuum and then get on my hands and knees and spread the carpeting yarn apart to pick out any trapped lint, justifying that my young sons were crawling and I didn't want any dirt on them.

I'd always been a mediocre housekeeper for myself, keeping the house sanitary and orderly enough. But suddenly, with the book deadline looming, I became obsessed with perfection as I cleaned the house.

Trouble was, the book weighed heavily on my mind whether I was writing or not. So housekeeping wasn't the escape that I desired. It was just delaying the only thing that can cure this form of anxiety: doing daily incremental work on the creative project (in this case, my book).

Once I realized that I was engaging in a fear-based game with myself, I faced my fears and started writing, and the book was completed on time.

It's the same way with any priority that calls to you. Answer the call, work on it, and feel the relief.

Part II

COURAGE TO MAKE A LIVING—*AND* A CONTRIBUTION —WITH YOUR CREATIVE WORK

Chapter Nine

The Courage to Visualize Success

You can overcome fear and intimidation about your creativity by visualizing success. You get to define what *success* means to you, such as:

- Happiness
- Freedom
- Financial security
- Public recognition
- Awards
- Self-employment
- Inner peace
- Approval from friends and family
- and so forth . . .

Visualizing means imagining scenes in your mind of your happy future, and feeling as if that happy future were happening right now. Top athletes, performers, and high-achieving people use visualization by imagining their athletic games, performances, business meetings, and other activities going great.

The Power of Visualization

At first, visualizing may seem challenging. As with everything else, practice leads to comfort and confidence. Plus, you'll have successes along the way that will convince you that visualization really works.

My parents taught me to visualize when I was a small child. Dad had resigned from his aerospace-engineering job so he could pursue his dream of working out of the house writing books and magazine articles related to his passion: model airplanes.

When he quit, our family had just purchased a new house, and my mom didn't have an income. We were a middle-class Southern California family in the 1960s.

Dad got work writing a monthly column for *Model Builder* magazine. He also created and sold blueprint plans for model airplanes. A customer would lay the plans on a table and then glue balsa-wood sticks into place to make an airplane. On weekends, Dad would fly his little planes at model-airplane events. He seemed much happier than when he commuted on Los Angeles freeways to his old engineering job.

One day, though, our family automobile broke down beyond repair. I had witnessed my mother praying over our car and even appliances like our washing machine when they broke. Her prayers always brought them back to life.

But this time, our car was even beyond prayerful help. The car had to be replaced. But how could we afford a new one on Dad's modest income? Some families might have begun wringing their hands with worry. But ours used visualization to dig ourselves out of the temporary hole.

Dad bought a model car representing the vehicle he wished to purchase. Now, with visualization, you can attract and manifest virtually anything. Dad could have manifested any car he wanted. For some reason, though, he chose a Ford Pinto.

Dad said we also needed to be specific on details. His heart was set on driving a brown Ford Pinto. So he dutifully painted that little model car, fine-tuning it until it was the exact shade he envisioned.

Once the paint was dry, he set the car atop the family television set. My parents called my little brother, Kenny, and me into the living room. They explained to us children that we were going to visualize this little brown "Ford Pinto" being our new family car.

Dad guided us to close our eyes and see in our mind's eye this very car sitting in our driveway. We were to envision that we owned it free and clear, without payments. Dad asked us to imagine how the engine would sound, the new-car smell, the feeling of sitting on its seats . . . all the details.

Well, within a short time we owned the real-life version of that brown model car. Just like we'd visualized, there sat the brown Ford Pinto in our driveway. My parents owned it without debt, just as they'd visualized, too.

How did this happen? my little-girl mind wondered. Mom explained that it was due to Jesus's promise in Mark 11: "Therefore I tell you, whatever you ask for in prayer, believe that you have received it, and it will be yours."

My parents, my brother, and I visualized with all of our senses, and believed that we had already received the car. My mom had prayed for God to send us a new car, since our old one had broken.

Immediately after these prayers, Dad got wonderful writing opportunities that paid well enough to buy the car. He didn't have to compromise his values to make money, as the jobs were all aligned with his passion of writing about model airplanes.

That experience taught me the power of prayer and visualization! So, when I was accepted as a client by the William Morris Literary Agency, I decided to put my parents' visualization lessons into action.

I thought it would be amazing to be published by Bantam Books, since so many of my favorite books were produced by that company. So, I took my old paperbacks and cut out the little Bantam rooster logo. I placed those little paper Bantam roosters everywhere around the house: on the bathroom mirror, the refrigerator door, my bed's headboard, and so forth. I even put one on my car's dashboard.

Whenever I'd see the rooster, I'd stop, close my eyes, and imagine glimpsing my name on a book spine with the rooster. When I had extra time, I took the visualization further, by imagining my Bantam book on a shelf in a store.

So when my literary agent told me he was sending my book proposal to several publishers for a "book auction," I was thrilled that one of them was Bantam. (This was in the 1980s, when Hay House had just been founded, and I hadn't yet heard of them.)

However, Bantam wasn't the highest bidder, and HarperCollins won the publishing rights to my second book, *The Yo-Yo Syndrome Diet*, based on my work as an eating-disorders psychotherapist.

But on my third one, Bantam *did* win the auction and they published my book about chocolate. Usually, publishers send authors a free case of their books prior to publication. But in this instance, I first saw my Bantam book under different circumstances.

My sons, Charles and Grant, and I were at the mall to buy some socks when we walked by a bookstore. "Let's pop in here just for fun," I said to the boys.

When we made our way to the self-help section, I nearly fell over when I saw my new book on the shelf. It looked just as it had in my visualizations! There was my name on the spine, with the cute little Bantam rooster, exactly like my visions!

The Bantam book is long out of print, and Hay House has since republished the updated version of *The Yo-Yo Diet Syndrome*. But it's still fun to relive my memories of how visualization kick-started my early writing career.

The Courage to Make a Vision Board

I'm a huge believer in visualization, needless to say. Those little Bantam roosters helped me stay positive and filled with faith. I've also created mock-ups of covers for the books I want to write. I place those book covers next to the desk where I write.

Another tool I use is vision boards, which are large pieces of construction paper or cardboard covered with images and words that inspire you. You can cut out magazine pictures of, for example, a happy couple, someone magazine pictures of, for example, a happy couple, someone with a fit body, the car you'd like to own, a place you want to visit, and so forth. These days, you can print out pictures from the Internet or a computer graphics program. Be sure to also include inspiring words and phrases.

Then, place the vision board where you'll easily come across it throughout the day. If you live with skeptical people who might deflate your optimism if they saw the vision board, then put it somewhere private, like your personal closet or an unshared bathroom.

Each time you see your vision board, stop and envision all of the images and words being true in the present moment. Remember Jesus's message, "Whatever you ask for in prayer, believe that you have received it, and it will be yours."

As long as the vision is God's will, you hold the faith, and you take the necessary action steps to follow your guidance, it *will* become a reality.

The Courage to Use Affirmations

I'm also a big believer in the power of positive words, positive thinking, and positive affirmations. (Affirmations *can* be negative if you're frequently stating a worry aloud.)

Invite the "butterflies" of ideas by staying positive. For example, regularly affirm, "Thank you for the wonderful ideas," or "I am *so* excited about the ideas that are coming to me now." Don't affirm negatively, saying things like "This is so hard," or fretting, "What if I don't come up with an idea?"

Several studies have linked self-efficacy to greater creative performance. *Self-efficacy* means that you believe in yourself, and you feel confident that you can succeed (Gist

1992, Jaussi 2007). The more you believe in your creative abilities and potential, the better you'll do. This makes sense logically. If you think you'll fail, you won't even try. But if you have confidence in yourself and in the journey, you'll keep going. This is where affirmations can help you gain self-efficacy.

As a mother in my 20s, I had the guidance to be a published author. My dad had written books, but they were all self-published. My guidance was to work with a publisher, but I didn't know how. I felt insecure about whether I had enough education and experience to be taken seriously by a publisher.

So I prayed for help, and God sent me a gift as an answer to my prayers. It was a book that I believe my mother may have given me, but I'm really not quite sure how it found its way to me: *Positive Imaging*, by Norman Vincent Peale (who also authored *The Power of Positive Thinking*).

In *Positive Imaging*, Dr. Peale described how he would envision and affirm all the good things he wanted, such as having his church filled with happy parishioners.

His stories reminded me of all the times when my parents coached me to envision what I desired. If I was caught complaining or speaking negatively, they would gently help me correct my words. When I'd gained weight in preadolescence, my mother taught me to envision my stomach being flat. It worked, and (except when I overeat gluten) it's still flat.

So after reading Dr. Peale's book, I decided to make a cassette tape of affirmations related to my dreams of being a published author. (This was in the '80s when cassettes were the latest technology.)

I knew that spoken affirmations in our own voice are the most powerful for intervening into our unconscious beliefs. I also realized that affirmations had to be positive here-and-now statements, as if our dreams were already a reality.

So I recorded all of my dreams, as if they were true at that moment. My affirmations included:

- *I am a best-selling author.*

- *I am successfully published.*

- *I am financially secure.*

I also added personal affirmations that my children were healthy and happy, that I had wonderful friends, and that my body was fit and healthy.

The cassette length was 30 minutes, and that's how long my affirmations went. I listened to the affirmations on my portable tape player with headphones two or three times a day. I'd listen while doing housework and while relaxing.

At first, the affirmations felt like I was lying to myself. I felt dishonest and uncomfortable hearing them, plus the sound of my own voice made me cringe. But after three weeks of daily listening, I started to believe they could be true. By week four, I was convinced that they *were* true. By week five, I liked the sound of my voice, because I learned to like myself through the positive affirmations.

Each one of the affirmations came to pass, and by the time I was 30 years old, I was a published author. I give a lot of credit to God, my parents, Dr. Peale, and those affirmations for helping me get published.

Chapter Ten

The Courage to Put Yourself Out There

Having a creative career means that people will form their own opinions of your work. They may tell you their opinions or share them with other people. Or they may just think them quietly to themselves.

The only way to avoid these opinions is to hide your work and never show it to anyone. Even then, you're likely to criticize your work yourself. We're often our own harshest critics!

Embracing Eccentricity

Most people aren't comfortable with change or anything that's unusual or different. Yet, as a creative person, you must present fresh, new ideas in order to be noticed. Along with being noticed comes the risk that you may also be criticized, feared, or misunderstood.

Frank Capra, the legendary director of *It's a Wonderful Life*, said, "My advice to young filmmakers is this: Don't follow trends. Start them!"

If you want to create life-changing, memorable art, then *you* have to be life-changing and memorable yourself. Shy wallflower artists rarely get noticed or remembered.

In business settings, you're respected and taken seriously when you conform to societal dress codes and behavioral expectations. In artistic circles, business attire is considered boring and unoriginal.

I remember attending a spiritual-healing workshop given by a male teacher. He was dressed in a dark blue suit, white shirt, and red tie, and the audience clearly told him that wasn't cool. He got the message, and for the next workshop, he dressed more colorfully and casually.

One way to blend both worlds is by pairing your business attire with one "statement piece," such as a large necklace, bold earrings, or a hat that functions as your signature. I'm rarely without my headbands, for example, as well as my oversize crystal cross necklaces.

Your statement piece could even serve as your "branding," in which people recognize you by the accessory you wear. Another statement piece could be your hair, such as an asymmetrical cut or an unusual color. Or, you could wear bright eyeglass frames. Shoes can also make a statement with a pop of color, such as my friend and co-author Radleigh Valentine's signature bejeweled shoes.

If you're still in the business world—and plan to stay there—you'll want to keep your eccentric clothing and behavior to a minimum. Choose one statement piece, not ten. The old adage "Wear your clothing; don't let your clothing wear you" applies. In other words, when someone looks at you, they should be able to see *you*. You shouldn't disappear in a sea of brightly colored prints and accessories. You also don't want to look like you're trying too hard to look eccentric, or repel business associates with overly odd clothing. Wear clothing that makes you feel at ease and reflects how you feel that day.

As we discussed in Chapter 2, being an original thinker, emotionally sensitive, neurotic, and eccentric are positively correlated with successful creative careers.

This means that you can't play it safe with your projects. You can't water down your original idea to make it conform with "normal."

You've got to take risks with your creative projects, pushing the envelope of what's been presented before. Even so, this intention can't be forced or faked in an attempt to shock audiences into noticing your work. Your creativity still must reflect your genuine emotions and thoughts, which means you're going to put your vulnerable, naked, and real feelings on display. All creativity is an autobiographical representative of the artist.

Will you be criticized? Yes. Will it hurt? Probably, especially if you equate approval with being a worthy and lovable person. Cruel comments still hurt me on those days when I'm tired and feeling vulnerable. But I use those feelings as muses to connect with others who suffer the slings and arrows of bullying. *Every* feeling can be used for blessings in your creativity.

As someone in the public eye, I now deal with being bullied daily with hurtful comments on social media and websites from people who misunderstand my work or judge me in some way. They talk cruelly about my looks, relationship history, and spiritual beliefs. Sometimes, I feel like running away and hiding in a cave. But my love of writing and my spirituality keep me going, in the face of painful bullying.

Just remember that all artists are criticized—usually by those who are afraid to express their own creativity. What critics say can affect your sales, but it can only affect you as a person if you allow it to.

Processing Criticism

There's also a big difference between having your work criticized and having your personal self criticized. If someone doesn't like your creative project, it's not a rejection of *you*. It just means they're not resonating with the project for a reason that's out of your control. Let it go, and move on to people who *do* resonate with your work.

Here is something else to keep in mind: There's a lot of scientific research showing that being abused as a child leads to heightened sensitivity to criticism and rejection. Adults who were mistreated, neglected, or abandoned in childhood often believe they're being criticized and rejected even when they're not.

This is likely because hypervigilance surrounding criticism was a survival skill to avoid abuse in childhood. Working with a therapist who has trauma-healing training can increase self-confidence, so that you stop imagining everyone dislikes you or your work. This may be an essential step in getting the confidence to complete your creative work and show it to others.

However, I don't reject criticism completely. I listen to it to see if there's a kernel of truth that I can learn from . . . and I have! Some people's criticism is actually helpful in improving your work, especially if you hear the same comments repeatedly. While critics can be cruel or abusive in the way that they criticize, their underlying words may contain essential truths.

So it can pay to listen to criticism in an impersonal way. Approach it as if it were about someone else, and see if there are any ongoing "themes" to repeated criticism. Don't bend your work to be inauthentic in order to please critics. But do consider whether the criticism contains nuggets of truth that you agree with.

I think it's important to avoid abusive and negative people. I don't spend time with those who are unkind or whose conversations are pessimistic. Life's too short! I hang out with visionaries, doers, and possibility makers.

When you're a highly sensitive and original individual, you're going to stand out as different and unusual. Even little children tend to reject other kids whom they view as being weird. It may be hardwired into our species to reject nonconformity.

So, know that you're taking a risk by being your true authentic, creative, original, and eccentric self. Perhaps over time, you'll learn to enjoy the attention this brings you. As long as you're secure in your self-worth, any criticism or rejection won't matter. You don't want to hang out with boring normal people anyway, do you?

Your self-worth comes from God. Being a child of God (as we all are), you are made in the image and likeness of our amazing Creator. Therefore, in spiritual truth you *are*:

- Creative
- Lovable
- Healthy

- Abundant

- Wise

- Forgiving

- All-knowing

- Loving

You can't undo, change, or wreck God's handiwork. All of these God-given qualities are within you. They *are* you! The true, valuable, lovable *you*!

The Courage to Deal with Family and Friends Who Are Critics

Sometimes, the people you live and work with are your critics. Their motives tend to fall into these categories:

- *Misguided protectiveness:* Your friends and family may attempt to "protect" you from disappointment by dissuading you from trying to make creativity your career. They try to talk you out of your dream, because they don't believe you'll succeed. They sincerely don't want you to get hurt or disappointed, so they tell you to play it safe with a predictable career.

- *Feeling jealous and threatened:* Sometimes, a spouse or friend may fear that if you become successful, you won't have as much time for them. They worry that you'll leave them behind for the big-city lights, that you'll find new friends or a new spouse, or that other worst-case-scenario fears will become realities.

- *Comparing:* Others may feel bad that they're not pursuing their own dreams, so they resent when you follow *your* dreams. They compare their free-time activities to yours and feel inadequate by comparison. Hopefully, they'll become inspired by your positive actions and go after their own dreams as well.

- *Financial fears:* Some loved ones fear that your dreams will cost them a lot of money. This type of fear usually stems from parents or a spouse who envisions supporting a starving artist the rest of their life.

- *Social embarrassment:* If you come from a "What will the neighbors think?" household, there may be pressure to conform to a career and lifestyle to impress others. Family members will criticize anything they believe will embarrass them socially.

- *Just plain meanness:* If your loved ones tend to criticize everyone and everything—perhaps because they're unhappy with themselves, or abusing alcohol or other incendiary substances—then of course they'll criticize *you*. That's just what they do. Pray for them, but don't take their criticism personally.

When I was writing my first book, I shared my excitement with my psychology supervisor at the hospital where I worked as a counselor. I expected him to be enthusiastic or give me words of wisdom.

Instead, I was shocked when he immediately declared that it would be impossible for me to get my book published. At that time I only had a bachelor's degree in counseling psychology and was working on my master's at Chapman University, in California. "You'll never get published unless you have a Ph.D.," he stated matter-of-factly.

I was stunned, but amazingly, I never wavered in my pursuit of being a published author. Although I respected my supervisor, I didn't take his criticism as *my* truth. It was only his truth.

I submitted my book and was published just after earning my master's degree. My critic would have been correct only if I had let his words stop me. I didn't.

Those who change the world are often misunderstood or underestimated by others. For example, the schoolteachers of Einstein, Beethoven, and Edison all sent home notes reporting that these young students were hopeless and stupid, and would never amount to anything.

Before Walt Disney built his Disneyland empire, his newspaper editor fired him, saying that Disney lacked imagination and had no good ideas!

Bottom line: Listen only to encouragement, not to discouragement.

Listen only to encouragement,
not to discouragement.

The Courage to Take Charge and Control

You won't get swayed by critics if you have a take-charge approach to your creativity. Of course, do listen for any themes that come up in feedback from others. If everyone says, for example, that your product packaging needs improving or that your book is filled with typographical errors, that's constructive feedback.

But if the criticism is bent on killing your dreams, don't listen to it. I'd also advise staying away from those who are hypercritical. At the very least, don't share your precious newborn dreams with a person who is negative or prone to being a naysayer. Only share your dreams with God, your guardian angels, and people who genuinely will be happy for your success.

Chapter Eleven

The Courage to Show Your Creative Project to Others

Creativity is half receptivity and half releasing, like the inhale and the exhale, each one following the other. It means that you're a conduit and mediator for the messages of the divine that pass through you, refracted like a prism rainbow through a crystal.

To put it simply, you'll need the courage to show your creative project to others—especially if you intend to have a career in creativity.

Treating your creative project *impersonally* helps to silence the fearful voice of the ego that quakes at the thought of criticism. This means, as I mentioned earlier, not defining yourself personally by any criticism.

i.e., my own

We only become controlled by the ego once we personalize the creative project, claiming complete ownership over it, and believing that if people like it, they like us—and if they dislike the project, they dislike us.

Yes, you put your heart and soul into any creative project that's worth its while. But the creative project is not you; it's an extension of you. If people like the creative project, they are liking the extension of you.

One of the reasons to depersonalize the creative project is to avoid the loneliness that can happen if we listen to the ego's seductive message that fame and public acceptance will give us recognition and a feeling of belonging and worthiness.

Yes, people who appreciate your creativity will tend to put you on a pedestal and give you high regard. But this form of adoration does not warm the heart like a personal connection in a real and healthy relationship. Public adoration is pleasant, but it's like dessert: it doesn't provide enough nutrients to live on emotionally.

What your heart really desires is a connection to Source, to your own Creator, to God. Creativity is a path of becoming aware of this connection. You are always connected to your Creator—all creations are.

So we cannot disconnect from God, but we can forget about our connection to God. This is when we start groping around for the feelings of connectedness through external sources, which don't have the ability to give us that lasting, deep happiness and feelings of peace and safety.

When we create, we become aware of the pipeline of pure energy connecting God to us. We realize that we have no "between" space separating us from God. There is complete communion and connection.

In each moment of pure creation, you are the recipient of divine inspiration. As soon as you receive it, though, it's time to let it go and give yourself over to the process of your creative project. Inspiration in, inspiration poured out.

Inspiration is the divine inhale, and expressing that inspiration *and* showing it to others are the divine exhale.

The Divine Art of Letting Go

Letting go is blocked whenever we second-guess how to express the inspiration, instead of trusting our first thoughts and feelings. It's also blocked when we hesitate to share it with others.

Inspiration is always flowing to you, and you're always learning and growing. So your creative project is a snapshot image of what you know about today. Tomorrow, the creative project won't reflect you as perfectly. But that's no reason to reject it. Because what you knew yesterday remains a true expression of yourself, and it will still help others who need to be moved by your creative project.

If you wait until your project is "perfect" or "perfectly reflects" your current truth, you'll wait forever. No creative project is perfect. They're all beautifully flawed somehow, just like mortal humans are unique in their own way.

If you're involved with a long-term creative project—like a book or screenplay—by the time you finish, it may not be an accurate representation of how you feel today. That doesn't mean you should keep rewriting it, because if you do, the project will never be completed or released.

Gustave Flaubert, famed author of *Madame Bovary*, whose work I studied in college, said it best: "I am irritated by my own writing. I am like a violinist whose ear is true, but whose fingers refuse to reproduce precisely the sound he hears within."

That's about as honest as you can get about the frustration of the creative process being imperfect. You do the best you can, and then you have to let it go. Nothing in creativity is going to be perfect. That's why it's an art, and not an exact science.

People's opinions about your project will vary, because everyone's tastes, likes, and dislikes differ. And *you* will be evolving and changing during the making of the creative project. So what you liked at the beginning may differ from what you like once it's complete.

Remember when you were in school and were told that during a test the first thought you had tended to be the correct answer? It's the same with creativity. Your higher self and your energy body are in complete sync. Your true self never questions the process of creativity. It simply listens and then passes it through.

Life is a series of experiences where we need to let go from the birth process through to our passing. Hanging on to fear blocks the flow of life itself. Think of a kink in a garden hose as an illustration of fear.

So, how do you release your creative project to others? I'm going to list some options and ask you to notice how you feel when you read each one. Your higher self and body know the best path for you, and will help you recognize it when you see it.

Here are some ways for you to release your creative work to the public:

Working with a Manager or Agent

A professional whose whole career focus is in helping artists can really boost your professional profile—provided it's the right person. You can work with both a manager and an agent simultaneously. However, it's not considered good form to have more than one agent or manager at a time.

My strong advice is also to review any contracts carefully with an attorney prior to signing them. This was a life lesson that I learned the hard way when I signed an unfortunate speaking and public-relations management contract without first consulting with an attorney.

When I broke away from the manager, I learned that his contract entitled him to 50 percent of my income . . . for life! I hadn't read all of the fine-print details, which an attorney would have instantly spotted and removed. I had trusted the manager and didn't want to spend money for a legal consultation before signing the contract. After we parted ways, he sued for the lifelong 50 percent. So, my publisher and I ended up paying attorney fees, plus I paid the ex-manager a settlement to undo that contract. I walked away with an expensive education on reading the fine print of contracts.

There are many types of managers and agents, including:

Literary and Creative Agents

An agent helps you to polish your book proposal or music and submit it to publishers. I sold my first book on my own, as I'll describe in a moment. The next few books, I worked with two top-notch literary agents at the William Morris Agency.

I was signed to William Morris simply by submitting a book proposal to them. I had no contacts or referrals. But I did visualize that they'd say yes, and I surrounded my book proposal with prayers and white light prior to mailing it to the agency's office (this was in the 1980s, before e-mail submissions). Within a week, a William

Morris agent called and invited me to a business lunch at a swanky Beverly Hills restaurant, where she agreed to represent me.

I was then assigned a wonderful agent named Mel Berger, who worked in the Fifth Avenue, New York City, William Morris offices. Mel submitted my book proposal to several publishers, and held an auction for the highest bid. HarperCollins won the auction, as I talked about in Chapter 9.

Agents usually take 15 percent of the royalties you receive. Hire an attorney to check the contract for expenses that they may also charge against your royalties, such as postage for sending you letters; paperclips (seriously, it's in some literary agent contracts!); mileage; phone calls; and so forth. You can negotiate these expenses, or even get them eliminated if the agent is motivated to work with you.

Agents for songwriters work in similar ways. (So do *talent agents,* described below, who book jobs for models, actors, and actresses and send them to casting calls for a 15 percent commission.)

You can find lists of literary agents, songwriting agents, and other creative agents with an Internet search. Agencies normally have websites that outline their submission requirements. My advice is to follow these guidelines, and have patience with the process. Trust that the right agent will be assigned to you by the universe, which is supporting your creativity.

When you're searching for an agent, it's also important to not be desperate. Don't say yes to the first agent who offers to represent you. Look for an agent who "gets" you and your work, and with whom you feel comfortable. This usually means choosing someone who specializes in your genre (style).

Although there are guilds and organizations for literary agents, the truth is that anyone can call themselves a literary agent. For that reason, do double-check credentials and track records of any agent you're thinking of signing with. Literary agents who belong to the Association of Author Representatives commit to a standard of ethical practices, such as not charging prospective clients reading fees or requiring up-front payment for representation without having sold anything.

You also may want to check out the annually updated *Guide to Literary Agents*, which contains the contact information for more than 1,000 agencies, along with an index of literary-agent specialties, so you can find the agent best suited to your project.

When I started out writing books about eating disorders and weight, I worked with Mel Berger because he was a specialist at this genre of book. After the carjacking incident in 1995, I began writing spiritual books, so I was transferred to an agent named William Clark, who specialized in esoteric genres. (William has since left William Morris and has his own agency.)

You'll also want an agent who'll work with your career plan. My first agent wanted to limit me to writing one book a year. As you now know, I write several books a year, so ultimately we parted ways amicably. I will always be grateful to him for supporting the beginning of my career.

Managers

A manager can book jobs or gigs for you. When I played guitar in a band, we had a manager who booked our concerts, collected the payment, and then paid us (less his 15 percent commission). As a speaker, I have worked with two managers who booked my speeches and workshops for a

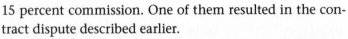

15 percent commission. One of them resulted in the contract dispute described earlier.

Normally, a manager will handle all of the marketing, the event details, and your travel arrangements. You'll only have to show up and perform, and then collect your payment.

You can find a manager by asking for recommendations from others who are in similar creative professions; by doing an Internet search for your favorite people who are in your chosen profession, to see if they publicly mention their managers' names; or by attending industry functions, like networking groups, clubs, and parties, where you can meet managers or their clients.

My first manager handled a famous speaker who was her primary client, and then she also worked with me and other authors. Ultimately, she realized she couldn't devote enough time to managing all of us, so she downsized to handling only her original client. It was a peaceful parting of ways.

Licensing Agents

Licensors help artists and illustrators license their existing artwork for commercial use. This can lead to very lucrative contracts with major corporations. Usually, licensing agents use their websites, and sometimes print catalogs, to feature their stable of artists with thumbnail examples of each artist's work and a bio.

Licensing agents can also help inventors, clothing designers, household goods designers, and other creators to put recognizable logos on their products, such as professional sports teams and famous cartoon characters. This makes the product "officially licensed." The product creator pays for the use of the logo, but hopefully the logo will increase sales so that the investment pays for itself.

In addition, a licensing agent can introduce a product inventor to a major manufacturer to have the product licensed and manufactured. The inventor then receives a licensing percentage with each sale.

Licensing agents generally receive a percentage of each transaction, which can vary according to the type of transaction involved. You can find a licensing agent through an Internet search, or by asking for recommendations from those in the industry.

Entertainment Attorneys and Talent Agents

An attorney or agent in the entertainment industry can help actors, actresses, and screenwriters find media employment. Usually, entertainment attorneys and talent agents are charming extroverts who enjoy socializing with celebrities and have developed relationships with studio executives. Entertainment attorneys can help you review and negotiate contracts, which, as I described earlier, is an investment that I highly recommend.

Publicists

A publicist can get you and your product featured on television, on radio, in magazines, on Internet news sites and social media, and in blogger interviews. Publicists pitch you and your product to media producers, and then schedule your appearances and interviews.

I've worked with publicists for many years, and have appeared on media worldwide as a result. I've also booked myself on several television shows (including *Oprah* twice). It really is a matter of telling media producers about you

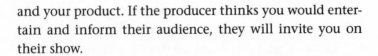

and your product. If the producer thinks you would entertain and inform their audience, they will invite you on their show.

Assistants

Assistants are full-time, part-time, or contract-labor people paid to help you with day-to-day tasks, allowing you to focus on your creative project. When I was creating my first card deck, *Healing with the Angels Oracle Cards*, I hired my son Charles (who was a teenager at the time) to assist me. Charles would go to the bank, grocery store, and post office so that I could stay home and write. Having the uninterrupted time to focus on creativity allowed me to finish the cards on schedule. Thank you, Charles!

I also hired an assistant who didn't work out so well. When I was giving a lot of workshops while living in Southern California in the early 1990s (when I was still writing and teaching only about psychology, not spirituality), one of my students approached me and offered to be my paid assistant. She seemed sweet and friendly, and she began traveling with me to my workshops. I soon learned that she was highly ambitious about starting her own speaking career.

That should have been a red-flag warning for me, but I didn't catch on. The next thing I knew, she had taken my mailing list without my permission and used it to market her own career. As we parted ways I told her, "If you'd directly let me know that you wanted help, I would have gladly helped you." But because she went behind my back with my mailing list, I could no longer trust her. Lesson learned: Beware of ambitious assistants who are only helping you in order to advance their own careers!

Being Your Own Agent and Manager

After all those experiences, I find it simpler to be my own agent and manager. For one thing, I no longer need to ask for work as a speaker now that I'm established. For another, being my own manager has been a case of "If it's going to be, it's up to me."

Every agent or manager I've worked with has requested that I rewrite a bit of my book proposal or has had to ask me questions about the title and description of the speech. It didn't feel like having an agent or manager cut down on my work time. In fact, it seemed to *add* onto my schedule, because I'd have long conversations with them about a task that would only take a few minutes to complete myself.

When you're first starting out in a creative field, there's a catch-22: Publishers will probably require you to have a literary agent before they'll agree to read your book proposal. This is to screen out poorly written manuscripts being sent to them. But the catch is that until your first book is published (or other creative project becomes successful), most agents won't be interested—unless what you're offering is so compelling and fresh that it's a sure bet to be successful.

With my first book proposal, I made certain to include a list of all the media that I'd been featured on and the speeches I had given. Most publishers—including my own, Hay House—are looking for writers who are "self-starters," meaning those willing to publicize themselves.

Whether you are seeking representation or prefer to act as your own agent, writers' groups are wonderful for receiving feedback, support, and direction if you're writing a book or screenplay. Most of these groups help you set a writing schedule, which you're more likely to follow if you know the members at the next meeting will be checking to see if you kept your schedule. A writers' group also gives you a safe place to show (and read aloud) your new book, which will help give you the courage to show your work to an agent, a publisher, and readers. You can find writers' groups listed in community newspapers or on the website Meetup.com, or create your own writers' group.

Endorsements

Do endorsements help in getting your work noticed? They certainly can! If you know any celebrities or accredited professionals, it's a good idea to ask them for written recommendations. You can also ask for testimonials from your clients and customers (either printing them anonymously, with first name or initials only, or including a full name with permission).

If you're cold-calling a celebrity whom you don't know, it's important to realize that their e-mails and regular mail are probably handled by agents and assistants. So, don't take it personally if you don't get an endorsement—or even a reply. Chances are that the celebrity never saw your request. Celebrities can be very busy people, too, who may not have a spare moment in their schedule to read your entire book so they can decide whether to endorse it.

It doesn't hurt to ask for endorsements, but ultimately, it's your creative product that endorses itself. In fact, sometimes having too many endorsements can make the project's creator appear insecure. <u>There's a fear-based ego energy in feeling like endorsements are your source of success.</u> No, they're not. <u>*You* are the channel of success, by pouring your heart into creating a project that will help and heal other people.</u>

Chapter Twelve

The Courage to Turn Dreams into Reality

A lot of ideas are discarded because the person can't figure out how to make them into reality and bring them to the marketplace. That's where manufacturing, partnerships, and networking can come in. A great example is the story of how Velcro was created.

George de Mestral, a Swiss civil engineer, was inspired after a nature walk with his dog, when he saw that nettles and burrs had stuck to his dog's fur. De Mestral realized that buttons and zippers could be replaced by replicating a two-sided fabric with one side smooth, like his dog's fur, and the other side hooked, like the burrs and nettles.

So he sought out a weaver to help him manufacture the product. He met with a lot of resistance from people who didn't understand the point of "Velcro" (which he named after smooth *velour* and *crochet* hooks). At one point, de Mestral almost gave up on the project. Finally, he found a

147

weaver who helped him perfect the product through trial and error . . . and a billion-dollar industry was formed.

Manufacturers

A *manufacturer* is a person or a company who can help you form your idea into a physical product. For example, if you want to design clothing, you can partner with a clothing pattern maker and a seamstress.

When my publisher, Hay House, approached me about creating a line of angel-inspired jewelry, we worked with a jewelry designer named Meg Hill and the manufacturer 1928 Jewelry. They met with me and sketched out my ideas for a crystal heart pendant with wings. I toured the jewelry factory to select colors and materials, and they manufactured the resulting necklaces.

A little research online will help you to identify manufacturers who specialize in products similar to yours. Many manufacturers of existing products are open to manufacturing other products. Simply contact them in a polite and professional way, and request a meeting.

Usually, you'll sign a nondisclosure agreement, promising that neither of you will steal the other's proprietary ideas. Or patent your idea before the meeting to protect it from being copied. You'll definitely get more information to help you know whether you want to move forward or not.

One important decision will involve ethics versus profits—for example, will you compromise on your product quality in order to lower the price? Will you insist upon fair-trade wages and conditions for the workers, which means a higher price point for your product? Will your product be free of harmful chemicals and animal testing? And so forth . . .

Co-packers

If your idea involves food production, then you can get help with a *co-packer*, which is a company that prepares large quantities of food according to your specifications. Co-packers follow your recipe and then package the food as you instruct them. Some co-packers receive a percentage of sales.

Distributors

It's one thing to make a product, and another thing to get it to stores where the consumer can find and buy it. *Distributors* can help resolve this issue for you, by professionally presenting your product to "buyers" or purchasing agents (the people who decide on store inventory). Of course, you can also ask for meetings with a purchasing agent at any retailer home office and be your own distributor.

A distributor is often called a *value-added reseller* (VAR), and you can find one by researching the VARs for products similar to your own. Approach that VAR and ask if they are open to distributing other products. If they have openings in their schedule, they will meet with you to discuss the uniqueness of your product, how it fills consumer needs, and the profit margins that they will receive on your behalf, with a percentage cut for their services.

Trade Shows

A wonderful way to show your product to potential retailers and consumers is through *trade shows*. Practically every industry has a dedicated trade show. There are trade shows for electronics, gift items, clothing, health food, books, interior design, fitness, weddings, crystals, New Age products, and so forth.

You can attend these trade shows to meet others in the industry, network, and make connections. You can also rent a booth to show and sell your product to the trade industry or to the consumers attending the trade show.

Crowdfunding

More and more artists, inventors, and entrepreneurs are posting their project on *crowdfunding* websites such as gofundme.com, kickstarter.com, and indiegogo.com. These sites perform a dual function of raising funds for creative projects and raising awareness about them. Many people read the crowdfunding sites for entertainment, since the ideas are so clever. People often invest in a project because it's innovative and they want to personally own one of the item you're offering.

Copyrights and Plagiarism Protection

It's a good idea to protect your hard work by trademarking or copyrighting your products. I learned the hard way about the importance of trademarks when people I'd never met started using my name in their ads to promote their own products and services. It's not fear based to protect yourself. It's akin to having an umbrella when it rains or shielding yourself by calling upon the angels when the energy is harsh.

How often is an idea plagiarized? Not often, unless it becomes a successful business. Then others will try to copy you. So you handle this with prayers of protection, trademarks, and the other methods listed below. But at the end of the day, your best protection is to create the highest-caliber product you can, with wonderful customer service, and let your quality attract opportunities and customers.

Here are some considerations to protect yourself and your products:

— **Website domain names**. It's always wise to purchase your full name as a website domain name, whether you plan to use it or not. I didn't purchase DoreenVirtue .com when I was just starting out on a tight budget, and then someone else bought it and I had to pay a high-ransom cost to retrieve the domain name. Do the same with your product, especially if it will have worldwide distribution. You might consider purchasing the domain name for each of the countries where you will be selling, and as many extensions (.net, .org, and so on) as your budget allows.

When I made the website AngelTherapy.com, I was still on a budget and bought only that version. As soon as my book *Angel Therapy* and my classes by that title became popular, others bought Angel-Therapy.com, Angel Therapy.net, and the extensions for other countries. I had to hire a trademark attorney to help me retrieve those websites, when it would have been less expensive to purchase them myself in the beginning.

— **Trademarks**. Similar to securing your name and product name as website domains, trademarking protects

you from other people using your name for their own gain. You can do your own work to secure a trademark through websites you can easily find with an Internet search. Or you can pay a trademark attorney to do the paperwork for you. Trademark attorneys are costly, but a wise investment if you plan on taking your creative work to a big level. These attorneys will help you protect your trademark from violations as well.

— **Patents.** Trademarks and website domains protect the name and slogan that you and your products go by, and patents protect the idea itself. You can apply for a patent yourself through your local patent office (contact information for which you'll find on the Internet) or work with a patent attorney. Patents are a necessity if you invent an original product.

— **Copyrights.** A copyright says that you control who can use and distribute the product. Usually, copyrights are for artistic works, such as paintings, books, photographs, films, and so on. Trademarks protect the name of a product, while copyright protects the distribution. You can register a copyright through your local copyright office (again found with an Internet search) or hire an intellectual property attorney to help you manage copyrights.

Networking and Strategic Partnerships

The old adage "It's who you know that counts" is true. After all, don't you enjoy hanging out with your friends? That's why people in all industries tend to hire and promote those they enjoy being with. In the business world, hiring friends is discouraged as a bad idea. But creativity companies seem to thrive on nepotism and having one big family of friends on board.

You increase your chances of success in creative fields by befriending people in the industry. This should be done sincerely, not as a manipulative ploy to get ahead. Creative types are sensitive and can instantly detect insincerity. They are attracted to individuals who have passion for their work. So be yourself and show your passion and enthusiasm for your creative project.

Most likely, fortunately, you'll enjoy befriending people in creative professions. Don't look upon them as potential competition; view them as collaborators, mentors, and partners. Don't allow yourself to be jealous of their success; instead, be inspired by how far they've come. If it's possible for them, it's possible for you too!

— Los Angeles, New York, London, and other major cities have **creative-industry networking groups** that "outsiders" (that is, those not yet working in the field) can attend. There are industry-specific networking and social groups for artists, actors, dancers, photographers, and nearly any other type of creative professional.

— **12-step groups** like Alcoholics Anonymous also have many highly sensitive creative members who are in the entertainment professions, including celebrities. Don't join AA just to network, but if you need support with your sobriety, you can make new friends who may also become your co-workers in the industry *and* find the joy of living a sober lifestyle. Once you get sober, it's important to surround yourself with other sober people so that you don't relapse with your old drinking buddies.

— **Volunteering** for charities that support the arts or attending art gallery shows will also introduce you to creative friends. Creative classes at your local adult-education center and community college are another place to meet highly creative people and those in the creative industry.

— The website **Meetup.com** is also wonderful resource for locating creative networking groups in your area. If you don't find the group you're looking for, you can start your own and list it on the site.

— You can also search the Internet for **seminars** that give you the opportunity to pitch your product to industry professionals. You'll have a set number of minutes to show your product or discuss your book or screenplay to someone who has the power to publish, license, or promote you.

— **Writers' groups** can help you with motivation and creative collaboration. While you may not meet an industry insider at a writers' group, you'll certainly gain new friends and valuable support.

Many successful creative ideas come from partnerships. Perhaps your strength is that you're the one who receives million-dollar ideas. Then you'll need to partner with people who have practical skills related to the ideas. Perhaps one person will be an inventor, another a graphic designer, and so forth.

It's better to partner with others and get your idea created, rather than deciding that you cannot execute the idea and then it never gets created . . . or, it gets created by someone else.

Networking and partnering with other people may seem intimidating, especially if you're shy, feel socially awkward, or have a history of painful relationships. You don't necessarily need a business partner. However, there are many personal and professional benefits from partnering up with people who share your vision. For instance, you can brainstorm marketing ideas, pool your research resources, offer emotional support, commiserate with each other, and share each of your strengths to make a strong business together.

As examples, one person may be the artistic visionary and marketer, and the other may be good with left-brain accounting and behind-the-scenes operations. One person may be great with social media, and the other has talents in making cold calls and pitches.

If you've been betrayed before, or have had negative experiences with friends and partners, you may understandably have some reservations about networking again. Especially if the project involves your delicate feelings, finances, and fragile wishes.

If you look back on those previous partnerships, you can no doubt remember getting warning signs that you were headed toward trouble. People show their true nature, and they do reveal if they're dishonest, unethical, or disrespectful, and have other characteristics leading to drama and emotional pain.

When looking for friends and business partners now, you're more aware and apt to honor those signals. Put the intention out there of finding mature, responsible, respectful, and ethical partners with integrity who have strengths and skills that they can bring to the creative project.

There's no need to rush into the wrong partnership, because the right partnership will come to you via your signals to the universe. A study found that creative individuals are more likely to be impulsive (Mackinnon 1962). This character trait serves artists who allow themselves

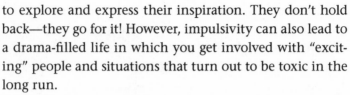

to explore and express their inspiration. They don't hold back—they go for it! However, impulsivity can also lead to a drama-filled life in which you get involved with "exciting" people and situations that turn out to be toxic in the long run.

Keep your impulsivity focused upon your creativity, and think twice before blindly jumping into relationships, jobs, contracts, businesses, and other life arenas. It's okay to say "Let me have some time to think about this" before committing. Then, do your research and talk with trustworthy, grounded individuals before moving forward.

Remember that when God gives you a good idea, it comes to you completely, including everything and everyone that is needed to put the idea into motion. But if you go into fear energy, you may rush into a partnership with someone who cannot fulfill the idea and whose presence blocks the right person from coming in.

Where do you find these partners? Mostly through the ether. Once you put an intention out to the universe, synchronicities are the boomerang effect bringing everything and everyone you need to you. You can also meet potential partners through trade shows, seminars, and networking groups in that industry, as we've discussed in this chapter.

Networking also can be your show of faith that you trust that the right person is coming to you now. So do put your feelers out there as you are guided. Just don't hold any "rushed" energy or feel worried that you can't find the person. Any fear energy will interfere with the manifestation of your right business partner.

Chapter Thirteen

The Courage to Market Your Creative Work

Marketing is probably the most difficult part about being a creative person. As a highly sensitive artist, you don't want to be pushy or bother anyone else. Plus, you don't want to focus on money—you want to devote yourself to your artistry!

Yet, as we've discussed before, unless you're financially independent, you need an income to pay the bills. Fortunately, you *can* make an income to support yourself with your creativity.

Even the greatest product won't sell if no one knows about it. You can't hide your light under a bushel. You need to inform other people about your creative project.

A few of my books have received amazing feedback from people who tell me that they have changed their lives for the better. Yet, when I stop mentioning these book titles on social media, their sales fall. It's "out of sight, out of mind," because most of us are so busy and distracted these days. Unless a product is right in front of us (via ads or social-media posts), we forget to purchase it. If I want to help people via my books, I have no choice but to keep "marketing" the books.

Here are some marketing principles to keep in mind:

— **Make sure you believe in your project or service.** If you don't believe in it, no one else will, either. Make some changes to the project if you need to, until you get excited about it and you know for certain that other people will benefit from it. Once you're excited about the project, you'll feel happy marketing it. In fact, you won't even think of it as "marketing," instead viewing it as helping spread the word so that others can benefit.

— **Make marketing a fun and creative process!** Think of marketing as an extension of your creativity, and have fun with it. Spend time making memes (those "pretty boxes" you see on social-media sites) that are themselves works of art.

— **Be bold.** Marketing takes courage, because you're asking others to buy your product or services. If they don't buy, it can feel like a personal rejection. So it can seem easier just not to ask. Yet, marketing is essential so that people know about your offerings. There's really no way around it. Perhaps the word *marketing* has a negative connotation in your mind, because you equate it with manipulation or dishonesty. If it's helpful, use a synonym for marketing like *increasing awareness, educating,* or *spreading the word.* They all mean the same thing.

— **Respect the sensitivity of the people you're marketing to.** This is especially true if you are marketing to those on the spiritual path, who are highly sensitive individuals. So, no harsh images or words in your marketing material. Make sure that your statements are 100 percent truthful, with no hype or potentially false promises. Keep everything as pure and high-vibrating as possible.

— **Hire marketing help if needed.** Marketing professionals include public relations experts (who book media interviews and send out press releases for you); marketing managers (who create and place advertisements for you); social-media experts (who create memes and ads for social media); graphic designers (who create business cards, pamphlets, and signs for you); and information-technology experts (who design websites on the back end).

— **Have patience with the marketing process.** Marketing studies show that time and repetition are part of the process. In other words, people need to see articles, ads, and social-media posts about you and your products more than once before they notice and remember you. It would be nice if you could place one advertisement for your products or services and then never have to market again. However, it's much more likely that your marketing will be an ongoing process. Those who are successful in the music, writing, fine-art, jewelry, fashion, and other creative industries are also those who work to keep their names in social media and the press. For that reason, set a consistent schedule for marketing regularly.

— **Make your brand or identity clear.** What is your main talent and focus with your creative work? What's your specialty? Help others get to know you. Teach them about your background. Relay stories about how you got into this work, and what your inspirations and motivations are.

How to Market and Publicize Your Creative Products and Services

So we've established that marketing is necessary. The next question is *How?* The answer is that there are unlimited ways to let the public know about you and your creative work. As a creative person, you'll get ideas about how to let your work shine brightly so that others will see.

Here are some launching places for marketing. Please supplement this list with your own creative ideas, especially in ways that blend with your brand of creativity:

— **Social media.** One of the most popular and least expensive ways to market is through social-media sites like Facebook, Instagram, Tumblr, Pinterest, and Twitter. Undoubtedly, new social media will continue to be introduced. Social media is all about being eye-catching, as people scroll through their news feeds and are bombarded with images. So be bold, while staying true to your identity and attuned to your audience's sensitivities. It's important to build a social-media following, especially if you want to work with large publishing houses and agencies who only take on those who have large social-media numbers. If you can't handle social media, you can hire people who specialize in this work.

— **Video-based social media.** Create videos related to your creative work so that others can get to know you and your artistic creations. YouTube, Vimeo, Vine, Meerkat, and Periscope are popular websites and apps to increase your visibility. These days, you can create your own television series or movie and upload it to a video site. You can even charge money for viewers to watch your show on Vimeo .com or get paid for ad views on your videos uploaded to

YouTube.com. Have fun with making videos, as I do with my weekly angel card readings on YouTube. They began with me using a little flip camera to record my hands choosing oracle cards. Today, my videos have evolved into mini-productions where you see me explaining the cards' meanings, and interacting with my many animals.

— **Articles.** Writing articles about yourself and your creative work is a great way to introduce people to your products and services. Articles are a "softer" way to market, because they don't come across as a paid advertisement. There's an objectivity to articles that you just can't get from ads.

Select online and print magazines related to your topic. If the magazines are free of charge to readers, that means you won't be paid for your article. However, they will publish your one-paragraph biography at the end of the article, along with your website and information about purchasing your creative work.

Magazines that charge for their publication are also likely to pay their writing contributors. So you may be compensated (depending upon how big the magazine is) up to $2,500 per article, plus receiving prestigious publicity.

Newspapers are always looking for lifestyle articles, either written by outside writers (that is, *you*) or where their reporter interviews someone interesting (again, you).

You can find lists of magazine submission editors through an online search or by subscribing to publications like Cision.com (formerly Bacons MediaSource) or HARO.com (Help a Reporter Out). You can also list yourself as a guest expert for media interviews in the *Radio-TV Interview Report* newsletter by subscribing to their service at rtir.com.

In addition, you can send professional brief pitch e-mail letters to editors, as well as television and radio producers.

— **Blogs.** What's on your mind? What would you like to share with others? Is there something you're itching to teach? Blogs are articles that you post on your website. They usually have a slice-of-life story, followed by a lesson that you learned and want to now pass along to others. It's common for blogs to have links to products or services you're selling. You can also post links to sites where you receive affiliate commissions. If you don't have your own website, you can post blogs on shared blog websites like Blog.com or Blogger.com, or be a guest blogger on someone else's website. If there's a website you frequently visit that features guest bloggers, look for a link that describes submission guidelines . . . and then submit *your* blog post for publication.

— **Radio.** There are two ways to promote yourself and your creativity via radio:

- *Hosting:* Host your own radio show either by asking your local radio station for a hosting job (which is what I did when I lived in Nashville, Tennessee, and had my own daily talk show on WSIX), or by using blogtalkradio.com or one of the dozen other host-your-own-radio-show services you'll find with a quick Internet search.

- *Guest appearances:* Go on as a guest on someone else's radio show and be interviewed about your creative work. You can directly ask producers to book you as a guest by sending out a press kit (a pocket folder containing your biography, a photo of you, an explanation and examples of your work, and 20 questions you'd like the interviewer to ask you, ideally). You can also hire a professional publicist to book you, or buy an ad in *Radio-TV Interview Report* at rtir.com.

— **Podcasts.** Record an audio message you'd like to convey and talk about yourself and your creative work. You can give podcasts as free samples for promotional purposes or as a free gift with purchase. You can sell them directly from your website or try to partner with a site like iTunes (even then, you'll need to market the podcast so people know about it). An Internet search will also point you to sites that promise to help you with developing podcasts.

— **Television.** Being a guest on television is a wonderful way to showcase your creative work to the world. Have the confidence to pitch your work with a press kit to television producers. That's what I did, and I was constantly booked (way before I was well known) on major television shows as a result . . . because I had the courage to ask. Or you can hire a publicist to pitch you to television shows.

Similarly, making your own television show has never been easier with the advent of YouTube, Periscope, Meerkat, Vine, and similar video websites and apps.

Even if you're painfully shy in front of the camera, your personality will help viewers to connect with you (they will relate to your shyness—believe me). Make your show about your creative work, rather than about yourself, and you'll feel more confident.

— **Events.** You can teach audiences about your creative work, or how to do similar creative work, by hosting or participating in an event. Here are some of the different types of events that are perfect for promoting your creative endeavor:

- *Workshops*, in which you teach for two hours or several days (or any length of time in between). Workshops are experiential, and participants get to join either in the creative process that you do or in something similar. You can teach at locations currently offering workshops, or rent a venue and promote the event yourself. (I recommend the first option when you're starting out, as you'll need help with logistics and promotion in the beginning.)

- *Speeches,* where you stand before an audience and talk about your background and creative work for anywhere from 15 minutes to three hours. Speeches aren't usually experiential like workshops, but are instead about the audience listening to the speaker.

- *Classes* that are ongoing, taught at your local adult-education center or community college. You can also teach online on sites like CreativeLive.com. Many artists supplement their income by teaching students how to paint, play music, write, and so forth.

- *Charity fund-raisers*, in which you donate your creative product or services in order to raise money for a worthy cause. Sometimes you'll receive a tax deduction for your donation.

- *Product demonstrations,* in which you showcase
  your service or product at a public location,
  such as a book signing at a bookstore,
  demonstrating your glass-blowing skills at a
  county fair, giving samples of your cooking
  at a store that sells your culinary creations,
  having an art gallery showing, singing or
  dancing at a community event, and so on.
  You can watch for events that would be a
  good fit for your mode of creativity and
  contact the event producer to see about
  working together. Or you can suggest an
  event to a producer or shop owner, or create
  the event yourself.

It's also a good idea to take speaking classes at your local community college or join Toastmasters International (toastmasters.org), an organization that holds meetings all over the world, in which participants take turns speaking in front of each other and receiving supportive encouragement and feedback to improve their speaking skills. Acting or improvisational comedy ("Improv") classes will also give you experience learning how to be in front of an audience.

My early adulthood experiences playing guitar with my bands onstage (including at my own high school dances while I was a junior) helped me to feel confident when I was called to give speeches related to my books. Even though guitar playing didn't prove to be my lifelong career, it did help me, so I'm glad that I followed that creative path.

The topic of marketing is broad and wide-ranging, and you can read excellent books and articles on it if you

want to know more. Whether you hire someone to help you with marketing or you make it a part of your creative repertoire, spreading awareness about your products is something that's necessary for a self-employment career in creativity. (Of course, if you work full-time for someone else doing a creative job, then it would be up to that individual or company to do the marketing themselves.)

Chapter Fourteen

The Courage to Accept Payment for Your Creative Work

To have a full-time career in a creative field, you'll need to have an income to pay your bills. This will enable you to spend hours focused on your creativity, as well as marketing and selling what you create.

Doesn't that sound like a nice life? Speaking from personal experience, I can tell you it *is*! I love getting out of bed, going into my little home office, and sitting down to write a book or create a social-media post.

You can have that life, too, or one that's even better and aligned with *your* dreams. It's just a matter of financing your life. Now, you *could* reduce your expenses and live modestly so there's less pressure to make money. Lots of artists do this, usually out of necessity. Some are supported by their spouses, so there's zero pressure to earn a living.

Deep down, every artist wants to share their work with the world—even if the thought of possible criticism is intimidating. There's healing energy within each creative work, and you naturally desire to share that energy to inspire others.

Artistic creating is a pure way of channeling divine ideas into physical form. It's sacred, and places you in the role of creator or co-creator. Through the creative process, you transcend the world of duality and go into the timeless space of nonduality.

However, it's also true that we live in a physical world, in physical bodies, with physical needs. And in our current societal system, money is required to fulfill these needs.

It can feel impure to accept money for your divinely inspired gift, and you may unconsciously block receiving it as a result. But if you need an income to pay the bills, your choices are:

- Work at a job and do your creativity part-time;

- Reduce expenses so that you don't need much money to survive;

- Accept financial help from your family or spouse;

- Win the lottery; *or*

- Allow yourself to receive compensation for your creative work.

It's a balance. If you create only with the intention of getting rich and famous, your creative work will carry that lower energy. Your sensitive potential customers will feel the "taking" energy within the product, instead of the warm, fuzzy "giving" energy they need. They'll unconsciously feel that you *want* something from them (money and/or approval), and they won't be inspired to buy your creative product.

Don't make your creative products your source of supply, because they're not. God is your Source, working through your creative products. As long as you faithfully implement the ideas you're receiving, and allow yourself to get paid for your work, you will receive all of the earthly support you need.

In other words, don't create in order to make money. Create for the sake of creating. Trust that the money will take care of itself, provided that you don't block the flow.

> *Create for the sake of creating. Trust that the money will take care of itself, provided that you don't block the flow.*

Creating is a process of receiving and giving:

- You *receive* a feeling or idea.

- Then you *give* this inspiration expression through your creative project.

- You *give* this project to the world.

- Then you *receive* appreciation and financial support.

The alternating giving and receiving is as natural as inhaling and exhaling. Both are necessary. If you resist either giving or receiving, you'll block your creativity and prevent yourself from having a full-time creative career.

There's an old notion of the *starving artist* that some have romanticized. Well, starving is neither romantic nor cool. It's tragic—and also unnecessary, with all the abundance the world has to offer. By allowing yourself to receive payment for your creative work, you *literally* can reduce starvation by donating to food banks and world-hunger charities. Plus, your success will inspire others to embark upon *their* creative careers.

Some people believe that if God gives you a gift, such as a divinely inspired idea or talent, you should give it away without charging money for it. That's fine as long as you have another way to cover your living expenses.

But if you're dreaming of working full-time with your creativity, you'll need to accept payment. If you don't, you may be like the thousands of talented artists who work in uncreative jobs just to pay the bills.

When you hold a job that you don't like, it saps your time, energy, and morale. It chews at your enthusiasm for life. If the work environment is competitive and harsh, then you'll spend your free time recovering from that toxic energy. Or the job may be so depressing that you turn to addictions to numb the emotional pain.

Any of these responses to working in an unfulfilling job will pull you away from your creative work. If you have the courage to allow yourself to be paid for your creativity, then you can quit your job and work full-time doing what you love.

There are old-time beliefs that we must suffer for our paycheck. Thank goodness these outmoded beliefs are on their way out! God doesn't want anyone to suffer, any more than a good parent would want their children to suffer.

You are spiritually designed to work in a career aligned with your passions. And you have the right to be paid for your time and efforts!

Don't you believe that a painter, a concert pianist, an interior decorator, an actress, and other artists deserve to be paid for their work?

Well, so do you, darling!

If you have been praying for abundance and financial security, the divinely inspired ideas you've been receiving are answers to your prayers. God doesn't just put a bundle of money down the chimney like Santa Claus. God gives you ideas that, if implemented, will earn your financial support. This is called *co-creating* with God.

The Courage to Co-create Your Creative Career

Realistically, it's not a good idea to quit your job without first having some savings or other income stream available. You don't want to put pressure on your creative output to be an income producer. You want your creative work to be purely motivated with the highest-vibrational energies.

Begin your creative endeavor part-time while still working at your income-producing job. Then, build up your creative work and income. Once your creativity-derived income reaches the point of paying your expenses, you can quit your job.

It's essential that you *value* yourself, your work, and your time. For this reason, do not give away your work for free—with the exception of small samples offered up in limited ways and donations to charitable organizations and events. Even then, you will receive something in return such as increased sales from the enticing samples, a free lunch for giving something to charity, or a tax deduction due to your donation.

Don't buy into the myth that you can get "exposure" by giving away free products or performances. If someone wants to hire you to act, model, dance, paint, play music, sing, or perform another creative service, they must pay for your time. Period.

When you raise your standards and expect payment for your efforts, you are telling the universe that you value yourself. And the universe will hear you loud and clear, and give you more opportunities to get paid for your creative work.

People respect those who respect themselves. If you give away your time for free, you are teaching people not to value it. Don't allow that to happen! Always charge for your time, and don't worry that opportunities will slip away. The "free opportunities" will slip away, but you don't have time for them, anyway. You've got a full-time creative career to design and attend to!

Once you go full-time in creativity, do not retain a fall-back "plan B." This means you don't hold the thought: *Well, if this artistic career doesn't work out, I can always return to my previous job.*

Having a plan B in mind will cause you to make it manifest. It's like when you lose weight, you need to release your "fat clothes," as a statement that you're not returning to your old weight. Make a commitment to your full-time creative career, and that's what you'll experience. You're not only creating artistic projects, but you're also creating your creative career!

~~~~~~~~~~

You're not only creating artistic projects,
but you're also creating your creative career!

~~~~~~~~~~

So take time each day to visualize the career of your dreams. Really, visualize the *life* of your dreams. This is how you co-design your future with God.

When someone pays you, the high-vibrational response to receiving the money is "Thank you" or "Thank you very much." Low-vibrational responses include apologies, putting yourself down, or expressing guilt verbally or in your energy field. This will disappoint the audience or customer who values your work. If you say anything disparaging about your work to a customer who is poised to purchase it, that customer will feel that they have made an error in judgment.

Stick to high-vibrational responses such as appreciation, gratitude (although not the overly cloying or solicitous kind), and sincerely praising the customer for their recognition of a quality product or service. "You deserve the best!" would be an appropriate high-vibrational response to someone who is buying your creative goods or services.

Allow yourself to receive with gratitude for, and acknowledgment of, the work you've done—even if that work was fun for you. Remember that suffering for money went out with the Victorian era. We're now in the golden age of instant manifestation and manifesting careers based upon our passions and interests.

So, if you had a great time creating the product that you just sold, *fantastic!* That means that your product is filled with joyful energy, which will benefit the person who purchased it!

The Courage to Sell Your Creative Work

Now that you've released any resistance to receiving payment, the next step is to actively sell your creative

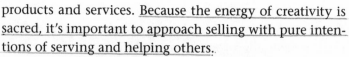

products and services. Because the energy of creativity is sacred, it's important to approach selling with pure intentions of serving and helping others.

Always think of selling as an opportunity to give. You are giving uplifting, emotionally moving, and other valuable experiences, along with enjoyment, inspiration, and healing, through your products and services.

When you have this giving attitude toward selling, you won't feel ashamed or embarrassed to place your items and services up for sale. You'll be excited for those who get the pleasure of owning and experiencing your creative work.

So, here are some ways to sell your work and services. This is a launching point, meant to inspire you to do research to find other avenues. There may be something unique in your city, or advances in technology may bring a new way of selling.

Self-Publishing

These days, you don't need a publisher, studio, or gallery to accept your creative work. You can do it yourself!

If you are writing a book of any length, consider self-publishing it as an electronic book (e-book) on Amazon .com's Kindle. Amazon has a free e-book that will walk you through the easy process of formatting your manuscript and uploading it for sale worldwide. Amazon's Kindle department distributes royalties monthly, through direct deposit into your bank account.

You can also self-publish with print-on-demand websites such as Lulu.com and iUniverse.com, where books are printed and shipped as they are purchased. You are paid for each book you sell.

My publisher, Hay House, also has a self-publishing division, called Balboa Press. They can help you with editing, cover design, and printing your books. If you sell enough copies, you may be eligible to have your book published by Hay House and receive standard author royalties.

The big benefits of self-publishing are the following:

— **You're guaranteed to get published.** Unlike a conventional publisher, where your work must be accepted for publication and you must prove you're a worthy author, with self-publishing you're immediately in.

— **Your book can be immediately published.** As soon as you finish writing your book, it can be published and available for sale. With conventional publishers, the process of getting a manuscript published as a book can take six months to a year or more.

— **The information in your book can be updated easily.** If you're self-publishing an e-book, you have the ability to continually update and change the content. With conventional publishers, you normally wait until the next printing of the book before any changes can be made.

— **You control the editing.** If you have an unconventional way of expressing your thoughts, traditional editors may not approve. But with self-publishing, you're in charge of everything (unless you've paid extra for editing help from the self-publisher). However, unless you're a journalist or language scholar, doing your own editing may not be wise. Even your computer's spell-checker can make mistakes by not recognizing a word that's spelled correctly but misused (*then* instead of *than*, *affect* or *effect*, and the like).

— **You receive the majority of the royalties.** With conventional publishers, you're lucky to receive 9 percent of the money paid for your book. As a self-published author, you receive most of the money (less commissions to distributors and any costs associated with printing and shipping the book).

In the "old days," self-published books weren't given as much respect as those printed by major publishers. These days, the snobbery is largely gone.

Similarly, authors used to flock to publishers because they offered distribution to bookstores, libraries, and other outlets for sale. A single author had almost no chance of getting a book sold in a bookstore chain. These days, with Amazon and other online retailers, distribution is open to anyone. You can upload your book to Kindle and offer it for sale instantly.

Publishers do provide the services of publicists with the ability to tell people about your book. However, you can also function as your own publicist or hire one (as discussed in Chapter 11).

Conventional Publishers, Advances, and Royalties

With publishing houses, you receive between 3 and 9 percent of the sales price of each book. So, if your publisher sells your book for $10, you will receive 30 to 90 cents per book. The larger the quantity of books you sell, the higher the percentage you receive.

Keep in mind that your percentage is derived from the price the publisher receives, which is usually much less than the cover price of the book. Publishers normally give 45 percent discounts to retailers, so your percentage will be based upon this discounted price.

Most publishers offer their authors an advance, which is technically an "advance against royalties," similar to a salesperson's draw on commission.

Let's say that you are given an advance of $10,000, based upon the publisher believing strongly that your book will sell well. Usually, you'd receive one-third of this amount ($3,333.33) upon signing the publishing agreement, the next third when you turn in a manuscript that the publisher deems acceptable, and the final third upon publication of the book.

It's exciting to receive an advance, but be sure to manage this money wisely (including setting aside funds to pay taxes on the income). That's because you won't receive any additional money from the publisher until enough of your books have sold to cover the advance.

For example, if your publisher nets $10 for each copy of your book that is sold and your royalty is 5 percent, that means you receive 50 cents per book. So, a total of 20,000 copies would first need to be sold before you'd be eligible for royalties.

Once your advance is paid back by initial book sales, you begin to receive biannual royalty payments for the preceding six months of sales. So, if you sold 20,000 additional copies (above the first 20,000 copies sold) between January and June, you should receive a royalty check for $10,000 in July.

So you can see that getting published is not like winning the lottery. It takes work and patience to make a comfortable living as a conventionally published author. Self-published authors who promote their work receive a steady income more quickly than those who must wait for a publisher's biannual royalty payments.

Websites for Artists to Sell Their Work

If your creative genre is artwork, such as paintings, drawings, and photographs, you have lots of online options to sell your products. There are print-on-demand sites such as fineartamerica.com and cafepress.com, where you're paid for each print that's sold. Other sites such as etsy.com and Amazon.com require you to create and drop-ship each product (or arrange with Amazon for them to ship on your behalf).

Customers can pay to print your artwork on merchandise like coffee mugs, computer mouse pads, clothing, keyrings, and necklace pendants on sites like cafepress.com and zazzle.com. Or you could do the printing yourself and offer these options through etsy.com.

Stock-photo sites like shutterstock.com and istock photo.com pay for photos, original artwork, and vector graphics each time a customer downloads the image.

If you'd like to display your artwork to the world, check out deviantart.com, artrising.com, and artstation .com (which additionally functions as a job site for artists).

There are also sites for illustrators, such as theispot .com, where you can upload your portfolio or stock imagery, which will go into a database that is searchable with keywords, making it easy for buyers to browse your work. There's a directory with contact information listed for each artist as well, in case someone would like to commission specific artwork from you.

Behance.net is another website to showcase your creative work where it can be easily browsed by potential clients.

If you are skilled with photo-editing programs like Photoshop, you can be paid to touch up consumer photos on sites like photofix.com. You're paid for each photo you retouch, and often you're given the consumer's e-mail address to add to your mailing list.

If you're good with graphic design, you can be paid to create company logos or branding via sites like 48hours logo.com, 99designs.com, and designcrowd.com. You'll work on speculation on these sites, submitting your design in a contest with other designers. You'll only be paid if yours is selected.

Wearable art such as jewelry and clothing can also be sold online at etsy.com or Amazon.com's handmade division. When I created my line of angel crystal jewelry, I was invited to show and sell the items on the leading home-shopping television channel, QVC, and QVC.com. However, after flying to the East Coast headquarters, I realized that the flights from my West Coast home (I lived in California at the time) would be too tiring for me. Although I appreciated the opportunity and very nice people at QVC, I had to turn down their invitation.

Videos of your artwork can help spread awareness of your talents and products, posted on YouTube.com or on video apps like Periscope or Meerkat with links to the site where your art is sold. These are also wonderful showcasing outlets for actors, screenwriters, singers, filmmakers, and musicians—as is the app Vine for very short video vignettes. Undoubtedly, new video apps will be invented in the future.

Other Outlets for Artists

Of course, physical art galleries are a time-honored way for artists to display and sell their work. Gallery showings make for exciting gatherings where customers admire and often purchase the paintings, sculptures, photos, and other artwork.

179

Festivals and fairs are also wonderful places to show and sell your artwork, including handmade clothing and jewelry. You'll need to invest in the costs of a booth space and creating your own display; however, most artists I've spoken with report making a nice income at these events if they price their goods with enough margin to cover their costs plus earn a profit.

Giving a speech or workshop related to your artwork is also effective. I know a mandala artist who presents workshops teaching other people how to draw, and benefit from, these sacred symbols. You can also teach art or music classes as a way to help others *and* supplement your income. Musicians can apply to play music at events and sell their CDs and T-shirts afterward. For example, my former band, Obsidian, was hired to play at the after-party of the famous Lavaman race in Kona, Hawaii.

As you can see, there are multiple options for selling your artwork, both online and in person. If you're determined to be self-employed as a full-time artistic creator, then there are plenty of creative ways to bring in an income doing what you love.

Chapter Fifteen

The Courage to Handle Ambiguity and Uncertainty

Part of being creative is the ability to handle ambiguity and uncertainty. Let's take a look at this now.

Abraham Maslow, considered the grandfather of modern psychology, once wrote that *mental health* means that you are comfortable with life's ambiguities. In other words, you realize that there are no guarantees, and that uncertainties are part of life.

Risks and Rewards on the Creative Path

There's no guarantee that your creative project is going to enable you to quit your day job and live your life as a full-time artist. However, if you commit to that path and spend your time and energy polishing your artwork and

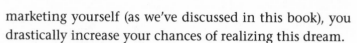

marketing yourself (as we've discussed in this book), you drastically increase your chances of realizing this dream.

I've met a lot of people who want to receive an ironclad guarantee from God that if they change their lives, there won't be any problems. Yet, challenges present themselves as we move forward and grow.

Yes, having a creative outlet makes stress management easier. But sometimes people who follow their inner guidance are surprised that they run into roadblocks. This can mean that they veered from their divine guidance and went on the wrong path instead of what they were guided to do.

Ambiguities occur when these roadblocks come up. For example, you may wonder: *How do I know whether it's a temporary problem, which can be addressed and corrected, or whether it's a sign that I'm on the wrong path?* It's easy to get discouraged if your creative project isn't immediately successful. After all, when we follow our divine guidance, doors usually open for us.

The answers are within you. If there's a part of you that doesn't believe in the path that you're on and then obstacles appear, it's easy to see this as a sign to change directions. But when your heart is completely invested in your creative project, obstacles look like tiny speed bumps.

Sometimes, these obstacles come up as messages from the universe that you need to adjust the project. It's not necessarily a sign to stop the entire project, but to "flex" it a bit. Often that's because there's a part of the project that is not resonating with your truth. Usually, ego is involved in that part. You were afraid of other people's judgments of you if you were true to your vision, so you tried to comply with what you imagined they wanted.

Life lesson that I want to pass along to you, which is a true secret to creative success: Never water down your vision to try to make it commercially successful. Trust the purity of the original inspiration.

Never water down your vision to try to make it commercially successful. Trust the purity of the original inspiration.

Rejection

When creativity is a strong burning drive within you, you have no choice but to continue creating. That drive was what kept me going when my first book was rejected numerous times back in the late 1980s.

I'd written my book proposal and sent it to four publishers, who all rejected it. Each sent a nice form note complimenting my proposal, followed by some variation on the words ". . . but unfortunately your book isn't quite right for us at this time. Good luck in finding publication!"

I'd heard of authors wallpapering their offices with rejection letters. That thought horrified me! Why would I want reminders of rejection in the place where I was creating? So I threw away the rejection letters and kept the vision that I'd be published.

Lots of famous writers were initially rejected by publishers, including my own publisher, Louise Hay, author of *You Can Heal Your Life.* Louise's manuscript was rejected so many times that she created her own publishing house!

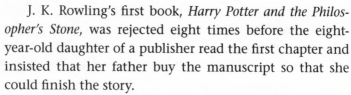

J. K. Rowling's first book, *Harry Potter and the Philosopher's Stone*, was rejected eight times before the eight-year-old daughter of a publisher read the first chapter and insisted that her father buy the manuscript so that she could finish the story.

George Lucas was rejected by studios for four years before he found one willing to produce his screenplay *Star Wars*, and look what happened!

George Orwell, the author of *Animal Farm* and *1984*, was rejected numerous times before he found a publishing house. *Animal Farm* alone has sold over 20 million copies. His last name has become an adjective, *Orwellian*, to describe being controlled by governments, which formed the plot of *1984*.

Before I mustered the courage to submit my book proposals to publishers, I realized I had deep-seated fears that I'd never be published. I was reluctant to submit my proposal, for fear that my dream would die from rejections.

I got in touch with feelings of being "less than" published authors, as if they were "special" or "chosen." I almost felt like they were *born* published. Who was I to think I could join in this esteemed circle of published authors? All those childhood memories of being excluded, teased, and bullied surfaced.

I almost allowed those fears to talk me out of submitting my book proposal again. I'm so glad I didn't listen to fear!

Besides, I now realize that if you're not accepted by publishers, it's not that big a deal. I mean, look at Louise Hay, who started her own company after being rejected by all the other publishers! And Charles Dickens was already a published writer but on the brink of bankruptcy when he penned *A Christmas Carol*. His own publisher refused to publish the book, so Dickens took what little money he had and self-published it. *A Christmas Carol* became his most popular work.

And it's not just books and screenplays that get rejected. All forms of creativity meet with critics who don't understand them. The inventor of the white correction fluid known as "Liquid Paper," Bette Nesmith Graham, initially showed this invention to IBM Corporation. They rejected it, so she began making the little bottles of fluid out of her kitchen. Although computers replaced typewriters, eliminating the need for correction fluid, Liquid Paper remains an office staple.

Similarly, an engineer named Charles Darrow created *Monopoly*, which was rejected by board-game manufacturers, including Parker Brothers. So Darrow self-published 5,000 copies of the game. They sold so well that Parker Brothers changed their minds and began manufacturing *Monopoly*.

So you see that rejection isn't the end of your creativity world. In some ways, it's the beginning, if you can channel your passion into making that product no matter what. Just be sure to listen for any patterns within criticism or rejection to see if there's something that needs to be adjusted.

As long as you're holding true to your vision, there's nothing wrong with paying attention to patterns within rejections. Ask yourself if you'd enjoy the product more yourself if these changes were implemented. Always be true to yourself. It's a great way to polish your product or service so that it's irresistible.

Every *No* Brings You Closer to a *Yes*

After praying and meditating for guidance when my book proposal was initially rejected by 4 publishers, I decided to send my proposal to 40 publishers simultaneously! I got out my *Writer's Market* book, which lists the genre specialties, submission criteria, and contact details of every publisher.

I went to the post office with a stack of book proposals and said a prayer that the right publisher would love this book. As I paid for the postage and the postal clerk took the proposals from me, I said a prayer to let them go energetically as well. That meant releasing worries and not contaminating the proposals with fear energy. I totally trusted the process of the law of attraction.

My faith served me well, as a sea of rejection letters flooded my mailbox. I kept repeating the phrase "Every *no* brings you closer to a *yes*," and didn't let the rejections bring me down.

What I learned is that books are rejected via mail through the self-addressed stamped envelopes that publishers require for submission. These days, with book queries sent electronically, the rejection letters come over e-mail, too.

Well, rejections may arrive by mail, but acceptances usually come via happy phone calls, as I learned after receiving such calls from four publishers who loved my book!

Now, a new "problem" arose, though. With four publishers all wanting my book, and me being unagented, how would I handle the situation? I decided to be my own literary agent and hold a book auction. Since all of the publishers were equal, I decided to go with the one who gave me the biggest book advance. Looking back, I'm amazed by my courage! Here I was, an unpublished writer, with not even a magazine article to my name. And I had the courage to ask the publishers to compete with a big advance.

Well, my courage paid off because they all offered nice advances, and I chose the publisher with the nicest. (Recall that the term *advance* means a payment you receive before you finish writing the book. Once published, you'll need to earn back that advance through book sales before you receive further royalties, as I explained in the previous chapter.)

So now I had a book contract, as I'd envisioned. *Why do I feel intimidated?* I wondered. Well, I realized the enormity of what I'd just agreed to: I had to write a book! The thought terrified me, and all of my perfectionism and memories of being teased as a child surfaced.

I worried that I couldn't write the book that I envisioned. I was concerned about disappointing readers and my publisher. Fortunately, I came to realize that I needed to focus on writing a book that pleased me, and to trust that the right audience would also resonate with the book.

If you struggle with similar fears, it's important to remind yourself that it's literally impossible to please everyone in the world. As much as you'd like to share your creativity with the seven billion people on the planet, realistically it's going to appeal to the people who resonate with you. And it's important to risk getting criticism from people who *don't* resonate with you.

There has never been any artist—not a single singer, sculptor, painter, writer, actor, dancer, or photographer—whom everyone universally liked. The top-selling artists have avid critics. Think about anyone famous, living or deceased. I promise you they all had detractors, but they kept going anyway. That includes the people who've inspired you!

The Courage to Stay in the Moment and Avoid What-Ifs

Going on a creative path helps you stay in the moment. As you are writing, painting, and otherwise creating, you are necessarily fully in the present moment. This means that you can only *control* this present moment.

Most of the time, it's my curiosity that is leading me. Whenever you research something, you then have ten more questions that need investigation. It's endless, and you never get to a point where you feel like you have all the answers.

This is where having the courage to be okay with ambiguity and uncertainty plays its role. There are no guarantees with respect to how it's going to unfold. You can only hold the intention to follow your guidance as best you can.

You *can* control turning off the television set or getting off social media, and instead spending that time working on your creation. You *can* control having assertiveness and letting other people know that you need some quiet time and space for your creativity. You *can* control that you will devote this time right now to your creative project.

These are examples of what we *can* control. What we can't control are other people's freewill choices. That's why it's a waste of time worrying whether your creative project will be "successful" or not.

Performance anxiety is when we put part of our focus on wondering and worrying what other people will say about our creative project. We imagine them loving or criticizing our project.

If we're not careful, we can modify the project to please imaginary audience members. When we're trying to please someone else, we aren't pleasing ourselves, and

Life lessons - changed quotes:
Everyday has its dog.

188

our hearts aren't in the project. We've diluted the main ingredient: our own energy and vision.

By focusing upon the intrinsic rewards of the joy of creativity, you won't worry about the "what-ifs" of whether the creative project will be successful in a worldly sense.

This is how you handle ambiguity and uncertainty with creativity: You focus instead on the rewards and blessings in the moments of creating. You allow the creative project to be conceived, nurtured, born into the world, and lovingly raised by you, its parent.

Just like raising a human child, we do the best we can, but we can't control the ultimate future for our "creativity child" (our project). To be fearfully obsessed with its future takes us away from the moments of nurturing it.

Financial Uncertainty

Creativity requires extreme trust, and the willingness and ability to be focused in this present moment. One of the main reasons why you may struggle with trusting and having faith is your strong wish to have your creativity support you financially.

If you're working in a job that doesn't satisfy your soul and you're only there for the paycheck and benefits, then of course you desire to have a career that pays the bills and fulfills you spiritually, emotionally, and intellectually.

Financial ambiguity can seem a struggle to live with. You have this uncertainty whether the creative work you are investing in today will pay off tomorrow.

One thing I've noticed is that when you work on creativity, your expenses usually go down. This is for several reasons:

1. When you devote more hours to creative projects, you have less available time to waste and fewer chances to spend money needlessly.

2. You feel more fulfilled, so you don't look for outside objects to buy in an attempt to fulfill you.

3. You start to care about yourself more, so you become more financially responsible and accountable to yourself.

Plus, the expenses directly related to your creativity are often tax-deductible. So if your costs go up for art supplies, check with your accountant, because once you commit to having a creative career, those materials may be deductible.

It's about having the courage to be self-employed and be your own authority figure, which we will explore in the next chapter.

Chapter Sixteen

The Courage to Be Your Own Authority Figure (Who Gives You Permission Go for It!)

It's a sad truism that artists aren't taken seriously until they begin to make money from their craft. I remember, when I was first writing, how much pressure I got from my then-husband to get a "real" job to bring in income. And, as I mentioned before, when I did get a job as a counselor, how my psychological supervisor rebuked me, announcing that I'd never sell my book until I held a Ph.D. (after which I sold several books with just my bachelor's and master's degrees).

I realized later that my husband and supervisor were both projecting their own beliefs onto me. They believed that *creativity* and *career* were opposite words. Many people still subscribe to the notion that you have to suffer for a paycheck, and that having fun at work means you're goofing off.

Another belief is that you must be a genius or at least highly intelligent to be successful in creative fields. Again, the research belies the myths. A recent study found that intelligence quotients (IQ) aren't an indicator of creativity, but rather that personality characteristics are more important. IQ plays a role only if the person is working on several original ideas simultaneously (Jauk et al. 2013).

Sometimes, our loved ones tell us that creativity is an unrealistic dream because they're trying to "protect" us from disappointment or financial struggles. They may also be trying to protect themselves from having to financially support us!

Statistically, very few people make a full-time living through creative arts like writing and painting. Yet, *all* successful people have creativity, which bolsters whatever career they're in. They creatively get new ideas for products or services, they creatively market their business, and they creatively give excellent customer service. So, creativity *is* practical and profitable.

Even though I knew the odds were against my being able to support myself as a writer, there was an inner drive that pushed me to write anyway. It wasn't about the money; it was about expressing what was *in* me. Yet, it *was* about the money, because I wanted to devote my time to writing instead of spending it at a meaningless job.

If people are pressuring you to "get a real job," let's look at some options:

— **Ignoring their pressure.** As long as you're not bottling up your feelings, you don't need to take on others' fears as your own. The exception would be if they are financially supporting you. It's only fair that you contribute.

— **Looking at the underlying reasons, if you're being financially supported.** If you're a fully functioning adult, why is someone else financially supporting you? Is it their own codependency? Is it their wish that you be dependent upon them? How do you feel about being financially supported? Is it affecting your motivation or confidence? The issue is complex and multilayered and requires a lot of self-honesty.

— **Assertively speaking your truth.** Tell your loved ones the truth, in a tactful and respectful way that you dream of a creatively based career. Let them know that this is *your* path to happiness, and you accept responsibility for your experiences along that path.

— **Making sure you're not projecting.** Is the pressure actually coming from inside you? Are you worried and pressuring yourself, and perceiving others' comments as pressure when they're not?

When you're pressuring yourself, make sure that it's love-of-creativity-based, not fear-based, pressure. An example of loving pressure is when you guard your schedule so that you have daily time for creative expression. Fear pressure, in contrast, is when you try to squeeze creativity out of yourself solely to make money or gain popularity.

When I was a practicing psychotherapist, I had a client who held three different Ph.D. degrees. She'd earned them to appease her family, who valued education above everything. Although this woman's true career aspiration was to be a professional artist, she was terrified to "disappoint"

her loved ones with a career choice that they considered financially risky. (As an aside, my client was in her 40s and was a married mother of two adopted children. Yet, she still had childhood anxieties that caused her to give away her dreams, for fear of her parents' opinions.)

So my client channeled her artistic love by taking numerous art classes. She told me that she'd been taking these classes on painting for several years, "in preparation" for the day when she felt ready to be a professional artist.

The only trouble was, she wasn't allowing herself to ever feel ready. She was always in preparation mode. As a result, she felt depressed, and she'd gained an unhealthful amount of weight due to nervous binge-eating.

I worked with her in therapy to take back authority over her career aspiration. She started to see herself as an autonomous adult, who had the right to pursue her dreams to be an artist. Her husband was completely supportive of her dreams, also.

Once she took back her power and stopped worrying about getting her parents' blessings, she blossomed like a flower: losing weight, exuding happiness, taking good care of herself with her diet . . . and, most of all, painting with the intention of making it her career.

No Excuses!

Being your own authority figure means that you take charge of your schedule, your creativity, and your life. As you've read throughout this book, you can be creative 24 hours a day, seven days a week. It's your natural heritage, as the creation of the creative Creator. In fact, you can't *not* be creative!

Sometimes you'll feel in the mood for creative projects, and other times your mind will wander. Let it wander. After all, your mind and feelings are always gathering impressions that will serve as creative bases. Just observe what you're thinking about and what you're feeling, as they are valuable resources.

Being your own authority figure means giving yourself permission to follow your heart and dreams. Of course, you'll be a responsible person while going about this, behaving thoughtfully toward yourself and your loved ones, and being mindful when it comes to your finances.

There's a balance here: Living your life to please others ends up pleasing no one . . . especially yourself. Yet, a self-centered life is lonely and can stunt your spiritual growth.

Being your own authority figure means having the strength to say, "I'm a creative person who makes the time and space for creative outlets and expression." You don't need to argue or convince others of your need for creativity. That's giving away your authority to someone else, like an underling begging permission.

"I could write my book, if it weren't for _____ [fill in the blank with the blamed people's names]" is a phrase I hear all too often. This is an example of giving away authority. It's holding someone else responsible, instead of taking charge.

Blaming is a cover-up for insecurities about your creativity. It's easier to say that someone won't "let" you have time or resources for your creativity.

I've also heard authors blame their publishers for not getting them enough publicity. They say that their books didn't sell well because they didn't get a media or workshop tour or advertisements sponsored by the publisher.

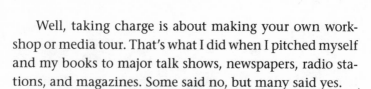

Well, taking charge is about making your own workshop or media tour. That's what I did when I pitched myself and my books to major talk shows, newspapers, radio stations, and magazines. Some said no, but many said yes.

Let's get real and be very honest with each other right now: The truth is that facing your dreams about creativity brings up very real fears about success; finances; criticism; your schedule and responsibilities; feeling inadequate, too tired and unmotivated to create, or ashamed; and so forth.

These are such normal fears that they each could be the basis of a masterpiece creation that could help others recognize and release the same insecurities. The key is to unmask them and look the fears squarely in the eye. This is essential to your self-authority.

So many experiences in childhood teach us to rely upon outside authority. In most schools, children have to ask permission to speak and go to the bathroom. Even in art, music, and drama classes, children are taught to comply with someone else's opinion as to what constitutes beautiful creativity.

I remember a high school art teacher insisting that there was a "right way" to draw, and me somehow having the courage to question her belief. Gold stars, grades, smiley faces, and praise are given to those who comply, and punishment is meted out to those who defy.

So it's no wonder in adulthood that we continue to wait for an "adult" to give us permission and direction before we proceed in taking action. Are you waiting for someone to tap you on the shoulder and say, "Now it is your time to express yourself genuinely"? If so, your creativity may be in a holding pattern while you search for outside permission.

Only you can give yourself permission to pursue your creativity. Yes, it's easier when your spouse and other loved ones are on board. But they may not see the value in your creativity initially. It might be after they see how much happier you are, or how much income you're receiving, that they understand. But all of those benefits can't arise until you first begin.

You may argue that you need money in order to begin your creative pursuits. Well, basic supplies *can* be expensive. But you know what? You are creative enough to figure out ways to equip yourself for free, or on a budget, as we touched on in Chapter 3. In the beginning, your supplies may be secondhand or refurbished. Have fun being creative with how you source your supplies:

- *Barter or trade for them:* In exchange for the paintbrush set that someone is selling, for example, offer to do portraits of their dogs.

- *Find them:* Use found natural objects (shells, rocks, leaves, and the like) or upcycled trash.

- *Make it a cause:* Partner with an indigenous person who sells used saris or handmade beads, for example. Your collaboration can be a fund-raiser.

- *Use what you've got:* Look in your closet or garage, and you'll find unused items that can be transformed into beautiful creations.

And remember: If you are motivated by extrinsic rewards, you're more likely to give up at the first sign of trouble.

Extrinsic rewards, you'll recall, include desires for approval, fame, and fortune. With extrinsic rewards, you give away your power to conditions outside of yourself . . . and therefore outside of your control.

A truly inspired work of art comes straight from the soul of the artist. It's a pure vision and soulful expression, with fully committed emotions and a statement that is clear. It's a breathtaking masterpiece, whatever form the artwork takes. However, if the artist keeps one eye on whether the audience likes it or not, this divided attention lowers the vibration and clouds the vision.

You might believe you'll be happy if you're famous or rich. While your creativity may give you these external rewards, putting your whole focus upon making them happen takes away from the inner joys (and *intrinsic* rewards) of creativity.

One of the biggest intrinsic rewards is increased self-love, which comes from acting as your own authority figure in taking good care of yourself. Self-care involves devoting time to your needs, including your need for creative expression.

Chapter Seventeen

The Courage to
Do Whatever It Takes

Like Thomas Edison's famous statement "Genius is 1 percent inspiration, 99 percent perspiration," it's not enough to have a great idea or dream of a creative career. You have to take human action steps to make it happen, even if you're feeling insecure, doubtful, and unsure of yourself while doing so.

Remember that ideas want to be created, and if you won't step up, the idea will keep traveling etherically until it finds someone who will work on it.

Many of the creative ideas that you download can seem, at first glance, to be intimidating. Many require stepping out of your comfort zone and pushing yourself to explore new frontiers.

If you don't know how to enact an idea and bring it into form, don't let that stop you. You have access to infinite research through the Internet, talking to mentors, and partnering with other people.

If you think you don't have enough money to create your vision, get creative! Get an investor, if necessary. Just keep going, no matter what.

The 10-Year Rule and the 10,000-Hour Rule

Studies of successful creative people have found that it took an average of ten years of steady practice before they had their first success. Researchers call this the "ten-year rule." While there definitely can be overnight successes, usually years of practice precede success. The most effective forms of practice, according to these studies, are when you are pushed beyond your comfort zone to a new level of skill (Sawyer 2012).

Every successful person had to learn lessons in the new skills along the way. I've certainly had to do that. When I have stepped outside my main writing genre of self-help to pen a novel, a children's book, and two cookbooks, I had to do more research than normal. There were times when I felt very insecure, but my desire to create the product exceeded my insecurities.

So anyone working full-time in creativity has to work hard to keep going in the field. Part of this comes from developing and maintaining *creative proficiency.* That is, to be really good at what you do. The old adage of "practice, practice, practice" really is true!

For example, researchers studied violinists and found that those considered the most "talented" were actually those who practiced playing their instruments twice as many hours as the other violinists. Psychologist Anders Ericsson found that an average of 10,000 hours of deliberate practice (pushing yourself to try new ways) leads to proficiency in almost every creative venture (Ericsson et al. 1993, 2007; Ericsson 2013). Further studies found that the number of deliberate practice hours was correlated to proficiency and talent in pianists, typists, athletes, and medical practitioners (Ericsson op. cit.; Krampe and Ericsson 1996).

Some journalists have popularized Ericsson's work as the "10,000-hour rule" of becoming an expert in any field. However, Ericsson counters that 10,000 hours is the average amount of practice time required, not a magic number. He also says that the key isn't just practicing, but *deliberate* practice, where you're pushing yourself to the next level of mastering your craft.

When I wrote my first book, I didn't harbor any notions that life as a published author was glamorous. Thank goodness! Because if I'd held any "illusions of glamour," I would have been disappointed.

For the most part, being self-employed in the creative arts is identical to running any other type of business. It means that your creativity is balanced by handling earthly matters like emptying the trash, networking, researching, and even marketing. It often means working harder, and also working longer hours, than in a salaried position.

Necessity Really Is the Mother of Invention

As I've talked about, an old saying holds that the key to success is to notice a need and then offer to fill it. Often, this is how creativity is sparked. Have you ever wished that someone would invent a product or service to help you with a recurring issue? Well, that someone may be *you*! This is how inventors are inspired to create their products and services.

As a highly visual person, I'll sometimes see images of beautiful items in my mind's eye. For instance, I'll see a mental vision of a book cover, an oracle card, how one of my rooms would look decorated in a certain way, or a lovely dress that I'd like to wear. I've discovered that these visions usually correspond to items that don't already exist. So, if I really want them, I need to either make them myself or find someone who can make them for me.

Necessity really is the mother of invention! As I look around my room, I see the shelf that I decorated. I had a music speaker that needed a place to rest. Not wanting a plain shelf, I envisioned an antique-looking cherub-angel wall sconce. I looked online to find one and came to realize that this item existed only in my mind, not in a store. So I purchased something similar—an unfinished white shelf with a cherub angel—and painted and bejeweled it myself. Now, when I see the shelf, I feel an artist's connection to it.

It's fun, creatively satisfying, and more economical to DIY (do-it-yourself) with clothing, home decorating, and such. It's also eco-friendly to "upcycle" and repurpose old objects into something new. I'll often add sleeves or extra length to my dresses with vintage fabric or parts from dresses I'm no longer wearing.

I also repurposed a book once! Before I began working with Hay House publishing, I wrote a spiritual book with another publisher. When I turned in my manuscript, the editor rejected about half of it. Instead of allowing myself to get upset, I put the rejected pages into an electronic file on my computer desktop. I liked the material, so I didn't let the editor's opinion dampen my feelings about my writing or myself.

Then, a few years later, when I was working on the book *Healing with the Angels* for Hay House, I pulled open that file of rejected material. I was delighted to see that the pages I'd previously written fit perfectly into my new Hay House book! And readers have embraced the book and shared how much it has comforted them.

Using Your Time Wisely

A few people have told me that they imagine my life as sunbathing on the Hawaiian beaches all day. Far from it! I write and work 10 to 12 hours a day, every day. Yes, I do take breaks to be with friends, family, and my pets. But there's rarely a day when I don't work. And my schedule has been that way since the 1990s.

I haven't taken a pure vacation away from work in several years. But that's mostly because when you're in a field that brings you joy, you don't need vacations. You don't feel the urge to escape, because you can't wait to get back to work! It's also because, if you're the creator of creative projects, you must be creating. It's not like I can hire a replacement to write my books. If my books are going to be written, I must write them.

Creative projects are like infant children, needing round-the-clock care and nurturing. Because you care about them, you don't mind. In fact, you thrive on caring for your "babies." And in return, they give you joy, satisfaction, and a sense of meaning and purpose.

If you find yourself making an excuse like *I'd love to work on my creative project, if only* . . . this is a sign for you to do whatever it takes to eliminate that excuse. Have the courage to try something new, to tackle a project that's intimidating, to research the best way to implement

203

an original idea, to partner up with someone who's got needed expertise, and so forth.

Doing whatever it takes can involve:

— **Avoiding distractions.** To have enough time to write, I must turn off my cell phone and the Internet, and put an "away message" on my e-mail, so that I can focus without interruption.

Like everyone, I have family and home responsibilities and concerns. But I've learned to treat my self-employment like any other job where you only take breaks at appointed times.

At a regular job, you couldn't take personal phone calls all day or go to the shopping mall for hours. It's important to treat your creative career with equal respect. After all, your creative project isn't going to magically be made by elves while you spend an hour talking with your girlfriend on the phone.

Similarly, you'll need to have boundaries with other people and teach them that you're *working* when you're creating: "No, it's not okay to pop over for a cup of tea and chat when I'm writing my new song"; "Sorry, I'm not available to babysit on Saturday because I have a previous appointment with painting my art"; and so forth. It's not unkind. It's treating your creativity as you would any other business. Because it *is* a business that will support you and help others, if you'll turn off the distractions.

— **Detoxing.** My creative career became successful and made me enough income to devote myself full-time to it after I detoxed from caffeine and alcohol.

Like a lot of creative folks, I justified my chemical intake by saying that I needed it to keep going. What I didn't realize was how much it was blocking my creativity!

Caffeine seems to give you energy, and it makes logical sense to think that you'd need energy in order to go after success. In reality, however, caffeine (and similar stimulants, like sugar) makes you anxious, fearful, jittery, and ungrounded. This type of energy is difficult to be around, so other people (including those who could publish or publicize your work) won't enjoy being with you. Stimulants make people talk too fast without listening, so your caffeinated pitches and interviews won't meet with success. In addition, the anxious fear from caffeine can diminish your confidence in yourself and your creative project. Caffeine also leads to insomnia, and you need healthy sleep to enjoy being naturally energized.

Depressants like alcohol and other mood-altering drugs (yes, including marijuana) can lower your motivation to work on your creative project. You get so mellow that you don't have the energy to paint, sew, write, and create. You also come across as hungover during pitches and interviews, which isn't the best way to win confidence from an art gallery owner, music producer, agent, or publisher who can help your career.

I detoxed by praying for God's help in reducing and eliminating my cravings for chemicals . . . and it worked! You can do the same. And as I've said before, there are free 12-step meetings (like Alcoholics Anonymous) in every city worldwide, as well as online. Your physician may also make recommendations for detoxing in a healthful and safe way.

— **An "I *can* do it" attitude.** This brings up the words *try* and *will*. When you say, "I'll try to make time to create today," you probably won't. Trying is wimpy and noncommittal. It has no energy, faith, or enthusiasm behind it. Saying "I'll try" has a defeatist energy of nonbelief.

Saying "I will make time to create today" ensures that you, in fact, will. It means you've made a promise to yourself, and you will keep it. Write your creativity appointment with yourself in ink in your calendar or put it in your calendar app with an alert to remind you.

In the end, nothing is blocking your creativity. You can do whatever it takes, if you're willing to.

Being creative is natural and inherent within you right now. But expressing your creativity and making it a profession . . . well, that takes creativity. Use your time wisely, express your feelings, and enjoy creating!

AFTERWORD

The Courage to Create
for the Sake of Creating

Creativity is its own reward, and creations don't always have to be directly involved in making money. Be creative for creativity's sake, because not everything you create is meant to be sold. Some creations are stepping-stones upon the path to someplace greater. Being creative is in itself cleansing and energizing.

Ingenious inventor Nikola Tesla said, "I do not think there is any thrill that can go through the human heart like that felt by the inventor as he sees some creation of the brain unfolding to success." Tesla must be watching happily from heaven as some of his inventions—which were initially rejected by an establishment threatened by his eco-friendly ideas—are now commercially successful.

It's about balancing your need to pay the bills with staying true to your artistic vision. The angels say, "If money is *all* you want, then money is *all* you will get." That laser-focus obsession with money will culminate in a pile of money . . . but don't be surprised if you also feel lonely while surrounded by false friends asking for handouts.

My mentor and publisher, Louise Hay, had me over to her house when I first began writing with Hay House. We enjoyed a delicious organic salad, freshly picked from her gorgeous garden.

I was overjoyed listening to Louise give me one-on-one lessons, and her wisdom is carved into my memory. One nugget that inspired me was "Never do anything just for money."

It made total sense and fit with my upbringing, where Dad had quit his high-paying aerospace-engineering job so that he could pursue his childhood passion of building balsa-wood model airplanes. He started a home-based business from scratch, paying all the bills and enjoying his life along the way.

Yes, you may get rich and famous from your creative project, but that's a side effect and not the goal. In fact, you'll make more money and get higher praise for artistic projects that are pure in their energy. With the population becoming more sensitive, aware, and savvy, people can smell manipulation immediately. They can sense when someone created a project solely to make money. This repels them, and the goal of making money from the project backfires. What sells are truly inspired creations, because they exude an energy of giving and sharing to audiences who behold them.

The key, really, is that we're guided to create for the sake of creating: For the pipeline of energy that's opened when we do so. For the catharsis that comes from releasing pent-up feelings through art, and expressing ourselves and being heard. For our hearts touching another through our art, helping us *all* feel less alone and isolated. This can also lead to success in other life areas, because creativity is universally therapeutic.

In my book *Divine Magic*, I discussed how we have both male and female energies within our creativity. Our feminine energy is intuitive, receptive, and right-brained. Our masculine energy is logical, assertive, and left-brained.

Together, your feminine and masculine energies make the perfect marriage in creating your creative career. Your female energy is the intuitive artist, and your male energy is the artistic manager and agent.

Creative ideas are like butterflies that are flying around everywhere. The feminine energy feels, hears, and sees divine inspiration. She invites the creative butterfly ideas to land softly upon her, and because she's so gentle, the butterflies are attracted to her and not frightened of her.

The masculine energy would want to chase and go catch those butterflies of ideas, and force them into successful creations. But that only results in the butterflies flying quickly away to safety. So you'd glimpse only part of the idea, or the butterfly.

Conversely, the masculine energy has no problem pitching ideas, marketing creative products, and enthusiastically spreading the word about the artistry. The feminine energy is more reserved and shy, so she might worry about bothering or offending others with any marketing pitches.

That's why both the masculine and feminine are equally important within each artist. A good method for getting them into balance is to practice giving three times a day and receiving three times a day.

Giving is a masculine energy, and receiving is a feminine energy. Both are necessary for mental and physical health, as well as worldly success in creative fields.

With creativity, as I mentioned in the beginning of the book, it's equal parts receiving inspiration (feminine) and taking action upon those inspirations (masculine).

When we give equal attention to both our feminine and our masculine energies, we become an unstoppable force of nature.

If you pray for help with your creative project, it will be given. God *gives* us ideas as answers to our prayers. When we *receive* the idea and it is divinely guided, there will be a sense of it ringing true, of it feeling familiar, and of it seeming *right*.

Then, you can move forward with the idea and put it into motion . . .

Or . . . you can talk yourself out of it because the ego kicks in and tries to take over. The ego most commonly will tell you that you don't know enough and don't know how to enact the idea into reality. If you listen to the ego, you will put the idea away and not work on it. Usually about two years later, you will go to a store and find that some-one else grabbed that idea from the ether and ran with it and made the creation that *you* were guided to make.

A musician friend once remarked to me that music, like life, is a series of tension and release. He said that all songs are a buildup of tension, with a crescendo at the end giving the ear relief.

It's the same way when I'm writing a book: There is a tension in the beginning of organizing many thoughts. As I mentioned before, there's this moment when the book gels into its personality, life force, and form. The time before that, though, requires a lot of taking action in complete faith that I will eventually understand what the book wants to be. I have to sit and write, even if I'm unsure how the book will turn out.

In the beginning the creative project is like unrequited love, where I'm courting the project and it's not giving back to me. But at some point, the project comes to life. That's when the book starts calling to me, giving me love, and chasing *me* with ideas demanding to be written down at inconvenient times.

So don't let it throw you that you may feel like you are working in the dark, unsure of your direction. Just receive and let go, receive and let go. This process will help the rest of your life that requires letting go.

Just don't let go of your *dream* to have a creative career, ever. The only way that you *won't* achieve that dream is if you give up.

A long time ago, I realized that the bigger someone's life purpose, the louder their fears. So if you feel afraid about not "making it," that's a signal that your life purpose involves creativity . . . and that it's poised to help the world in a big way.

Think of all of the creative books, art, inventions, and other products that have helped you. Aren't you grateful that the people who had those ideas pursued them? It's virtually guaranteed that they overcame insecurities and other obstacles to get their creations into form.

Don't let little disappointments distract you from the bigger picture. Keep your sights focused upon the divine light within your creativity. Never compare yourself to others, and keep the faith.

You already *are* courageous, and you were born to create!

With love,

Doreen

BIBLIOGRAPHY

Alfonso, C. A., and Wellington, A. (2002 Winter). Dreams and creativity—collaborative psychoanalytic work. *J Am Acad Psychoanal.* 30(4): 573–82.

Aronson, E., Willerman, B., and Floyd, J. (1966). The effect of a pratfall on increasing interpersonal attractiveness. *Psychonomic Science.* 4: 227–8.

Bar-Sela, G., et. al. (2007). Art therapy improved depression and influenced fatigue levels in cancer patients on chemotherapy. *Psycho-Oncology.* 16(11).

Bauer, M., et. al. (2014). Relationship between sunlight and the age of onset of bipolar disorder: An international multisite study. *J Affect Disord.* 67: 104–11.

Beijamini, F., et. al. (2014 Jan 8). After being challenged by a video game problem, sleep increases the chance to solve it. *PLoS One.* 9(1).

Benedetti, F., Colombo, C., Barbini, B., Campori, E., and Smeraldi, E. (2001 Feb). Morning sunlight reduces length of hospitalization in bipolar depression. *J Affect Disord.* 62(3):221–3.

Bolte, A., Goschke, T., and Kuhl, J. (2003). Emotion and intuition: Effects of positive and negative mood on implicit judgments of semantic coherence. *Psychological Science.* 14(5): 416–21.

Csikszentmihalyi, M. (1990). *Flow: The Psychology of Optimal Experience.* New York: Harper & Row.

Ding, X., Tang, Y. Y., Tang, R., and Posner, M. I. (2014 Mar 19). Improving creativity performance by short-term meditation. *Behav Brain Funct.* 10: 9.

Eaton, L. G., et. al. (2007). A review of research and methods used to establish art therapy as an effective treatment method for traumatized children. *The Arts in Psychotherapy.* 34(3): 256–62.

Ericsson, K. A. (2013 Jun). Training history, deliberate practice and elite sports performance: An analysis in response to Tucker and Collins review—what makes champions? *Br J Sports Med.* 47(9): 533–5.

Ericsson, K. A., Prietula, M. J., and Cokely, E. T. (2007 Jul–Aug). The making of an expert. *Harv Bus Rev.* 85(7-8): 114–21, 193.

Ericsson, K. A., Krampe, R. T., and Heizmann, S. (1993). Can we create gifted people? *Ciba Found Symp.* 178: 222–31; discussion 232–49.

Gardner, A. (2013 Sep 25). "Power naps" may boost right-brain activity. CNN Health. Retrieved from: http://www.cnn.com/2012/10/17/health/health-naps-brain/index.html.

Gist, M. E., and Mitchell, T. R. (1992). Self-efficacy: A theoretical analysis of its determinants and malleability. *Academy of Management Review.* 17(2): 183–211, quoted in Sawyer, op.cit.

Gridley, M. C. (2004 Apr). Myers-Briggs personality types of art collectors. *Psychol Rep.* 94(2): 736–8.

Gruber, H. E., and Davis, S. N. (1988). Inching our way up Mount Olympus: The evolving-systems approach to creative thinking. In R. J. Sternberg, ed. *The Nature of Creativity.* New York: Cambridge University Press: 243–70, quoted in Sawyer, op.cit.

Hellbom, E. (2014). Intuition, a part of bipolar disorder? The emotional brain-survival and time. *Open Journal of Depression.* 3: 41–4.

Helmreich, R., Aronson, E., and LeFan, J. (1970). To err is humanizing sometimes: Effects of self-esteem, competence, and a pratfall on interpersonal attraction. *Journal of Personality and Social Psychology.* 16(2): 259.

Isen, A. M. (1998). On the relationship between affect and creative problem solving. In S. W. Russ, ed., *Affect, Creative Experience, and Psychological Adjustment.* Philadelphia: Brunner/Mazel: 3–17.

———. (1999). Positive affect. In T. Dalgleish and M. Power, eds. *Handbook of Cognition and Emotion.* New York: John Wiley & Sons: 522–39.

Ives-Deliperi, V. L., Howells F., Stein, D. J., Meintjes, E. M., and Horn, N. (2013 Sep 25). The effects of mindfulness-based cognitive therapy in patients with bipolar disorder: a controlled functional MRI investigation. *J Affect Disord.* 150(3): 1152–7.

Jacka, F. N., Pasco, J. A., Mykletun, A., Williams, L. J., Nicholson, G. C., Kotowicz, M. A., and Berk, M. (2011 Mar). Diet quality in bipolar disorder in a population-based sample of women. *J Affect Disord.* 129(1-3): 332–7.

Janka, Z. (2004 Aug 15). Artistic creativity and bipolar mood disorder. *Orv Hetil*. 145(33): 1709–18.

Jauk, E., Benedek, M., Dunst, B., and Neubauer, A. C. (2013 Jul). The relationship between intelligence and creativity: New support for the threshold hypothesis by means of empirical breakpoint detection. *Intelligence*. 41(4): 212–21.

Jaussi, K.S., et. al. (2007). I am, I think I can, and I do: The role of personal identity, self-efficacy, and cross-application of experiences in creativity at work. *Creativity Research Journal*. 19: 247–258, quoted in Sawyer, op.cit.

Kent, S. T., McClure, L. A., Crosson, W. L., Arnett, D. K., Wadley, V. G., and Sathiakumar, N. (2009 Jul 28). Effect of sunlight exposure on cognitive function among depressed and non-depressed participants: A REGARDS cross-sectional study. *Environ Health*. 8: 34.

Koris, S. (1980 Nov 24). Sci-fi, of course, but Ray Bradbury's literary exploits go well beyond either science or fiction. *People*. 14(21). Retrieved from: http://www.people.com/people/archive/article/0,,20077947,00.html.

Krampe, R. T., and Ericsson, K. A. (1996 Dec). Maintaining excellence: deliberate practice and elite performance in young and older pianists. *J Exp Psychol Gen*. 125(4): 331–59.

Leung, A. K. (2014 Oct). The role of instrumental emotion regulation in the emotions-creativity link: How worries render individuals with high neuroticism more creative. *Emotion*. 14(5): 846–56.

Lewis, C. S. (1966). It all began with a picture. In Walter Hooper, ed. *Of Other Worlds: Essays and Stories*. London: Geoffrey Bles: 42–3.

Mackinnon, D. W. (1962 Jul). The nature and nurture of creative talent. *American Psychologist*. 17(7): 484–95.

Maremmani, I., Perugi, G., Rovai, L., Maremmani, A. G., Pacini, M., Canonico, P. L., Carbonato, P., Mencacci, C., Muscettola, G., Pani, L., Torta, R., Vampini, C., and Akiskal, H. S. (2011 Sep). Are "social drugs" (tobacco, coffee and chocolate) related to the bipolar spectrum? *J Affect Disord*. (1-2): 227–33.

McCraty, R., Atkinson, M., Tomasino, D., and Bradley, R. T. (2006). *The Coherent Heart: Heart–Brain Interactions, Psychophysiological Coherence, and the Emergence of System-Wide Order*. Boulder Creek, CA: HeartMath Research Center, Institute of HeartMath.

McCrea, S. M. (2010). Intuition, insight, and the right hemisphere: Emergence of higher sociocognitive functions. *Psychol Res Behav Manag.* 3: 1–39.

Puetz, T. W. (2013 Jun 10). Effects of creative arts therapies on psychological symptoms and quality of life in patients with cancer. *JAMA Intern Med.* 173(11).

"Ray Bradbury." *Day at Night.* James Day, host. Public Television. Original tape date: January 21, 1974. Retrieved from: http://www.cuny.tv/show/dayatnight/PR1012346.

Sawyer, R. K. (2012). *Explaining Creativity: The Science of Human Innovation.* New York: Oxford University Press.

Schouten, K. A. (2015 Apr). The effectiveness of art therapy in the treatment of traumatized adults: A systematic review on art therapy and trauma. *Trauma Violence Abuse.* 16(2): 220–8.

Soreca, I. (2014 Nov). Circadian rhythms and sleep in bipolar disorder: Implications for pathophysiology and treatment. *Curr Opin Psychiatry.* 27(6): 467–71.

Strayer, D. (2012 Dec 12). Nature nurtures creativity: Hikers more inspired on tests after four days unplugged. *U News Center.* University of Utah. Retrieved from: http://archive.unews.utah.edu/news_releases/nature-nurtures-creativity-2.

Tomasino, D. (2007). The psychophysiological basis of creativity and intuition: Accessing "The Zone" of entrepreneurship. *Int. J. Entrepreneurship and Small Business.* 4(5).

Uebelacker, L. A., Weinstock, L. M., and Kraines, M. A. (2014 Sep). Self-reported benefits and risks of yoga in individuals with bipolar disorder. *J Psychiatr Pract.* 20(5): 345–52.

Walton-Moss, B., Ray, E. M., and Woodruff, K. (2013 Oct–Dec). Relationship of spirituality or religion to recovery from substance abuse: a systematic review. *J Addict Nurs.* 24(4): 217–26.

Zaslaw, N. (1994). Mozart as a working stiff. In James M. Morris, ed. *On Mozart.* Cambridge, U.K.: Cambridge University Press.

ABOUT THE AUTHOR

Doreen Virtue holds B.A., M.A., and Ph.D. degrees in counseling psychology and is a lifelong clairvoyant and Christian mystic. A former psychotherapist, Doreen now gives online workshops on topics related to her books and oracle cards. She's the author of *Assertiveness for Earth Angels, Don't Let Anything Dull Your Sparkle, The Miracles of Archangel Michael,* and *Archangel Oracle Cards,* among many other works. She has appeared on *Oprah,* CNN, the BBC, *The View,* and *Good Morning America* and has been featured in newspapers and magazines worldwide. For information on Doreen's work, please visit her at AngelTherapy.com or Facebook.com/DoreenVirtue444. To enroll in Doreen's video courses, please visit www.HayHouseUniversity.com and www.EarthAngel.com.

Hay House Titles of Related Interest

We hope you enjoyed this Hay House book. If you'd like to receive our online catalog featuring additional information on ay House books and products, or if you'd like to find out more about the Hay Foundation, please contact:

Hay House, Inc., P.O. Box 5100, Carlsbad, CA 92018-5100
(760) 431-7695 or (800) 654-5126
(760) 431-6948 (fax) or (800) 650-5115 (fax)
www.hayhouse.com® • www.hayfoundation.org

✦

Published and distributed in Australia by:
Hay House Australia Pty. Ltd., 18/36 Ralph St., Alexandria NSW 2015
Phone: 612-9669-4299 • *Fax:* 612-9669-4144 • www.hayhouse.com.au

Published and distributed in the United Kingdom by:
Hay House UK, Ltd., Astley House, 33 Notting Hill Gate, London W11 3JQ
Phone: 44-20-3675-2450 • *Fax:* 44-20-3675-2451 • www.hayhouse.co.uk

Published and distributed in the Republic of South Africa by:
Hay House SA (Pty), Ltd., P.O. Box 990, Witkoppen 2068
info@hayhouse.co.za • www.hayhouse.co.za

Published in India by: Hay House Publishers India,
Muskaan Complex, Plot No. 3, B-2, Vasant Kunj, New Delhi 110 070
Phone: 91-11-4176-1620 • *Fax:* 91-11-4176-1630 • www.hayhouse.co.in

Distributed in Canada by: Raincoast Books,
2440 Viking Way, Richmond, B.C. V6V 1N2
Phone: 1-800-663-5714 • *Fax:* 1-800-565-3770 • www.raincoast.com

✦

Take Your Soul on a Vacation

Visit www.HealYourLife.com® to regroup,
recharge, and reconnect with your own magnificence.
Featuring blogs, mind-body-spirit news, and
life-changing wisdom from Louise Hay and friends.

Visit www.HealYourLife.com today!